The GREAT TRAIN ROBBERY
and other RAILWAY CRIMES

The GREAT TRAIN ROBBERY
and other RAILWAY CRIMES

Mike Holgate

HALSGROVE

First published in Great Britain in 2013

British Library Cataloguing-in-Publication Data
A CIP record for this title is available from the British Library

ISBN 978 0 85704 202 6

HALSGROVE
Halsgrove House,
Ryelands Business Park,
Bagley Road, Wellington, Somerset TA21 9PZ
Tel: 01823 653777   Fax: 01823 216796
email: sales@halsgrove.com

Part of the Halsgrove group of companies
Information on all Halsgrove titles is available at:
www.halsgrove.com

Printed in China by Everbest Printing Co Ltd

CONTENTS

'The Modern Dick Turpin' by US artist Edward Penfield. In Britain, highwaymen turned their attention to trains long before the first railway robbery in America.

ACKNOWLEDGEMENTS

The author would like to extend his grateful thanks to Torbay Libraries for access to antiquarian books, magazines, newspapers and online resources. Images obtained from Torbay Libraries supplemented online sources and the collection of the author. The pictures selected were mainly published in contemporary journals and periodicals including: *The Graphic, Harper's News, The Illustrated London News, Illustrated Police News, Penny Illustrated.*

When the train thieves struck on New Year's Day
A fortune in valuables went astray
It was the most audacious crime
The Great Train Robbery of 1849

Bullion thieves could have got clean away
Instead they were sent to Botany Bay
Transported overseas for life
The Great Train Robbery of 1855

Millions were stolen from a royal mail train
Brought to a halt by a signal change
The most infamous crime of the century
The Great Train Robbery of 1963

INTRODUCTION

Having previously written books examining various aspects of the Great Train Robbery and the Whitechapel Murders, it occurred to me that significant anniversaries occurring this year presented a unique opportunity to produce a work combining the two most infamous crimes in history. In August 2013, it will be fifty years since the 1963 train robbery considered the greatest crime of the Twentieth Century and 125 years since the capital's infamous serial killer, Jack the Ripper, considered by one expert to be a railway employee, first struck in 1888.

In addition, 2013 marks the 175th anniversary of the Coronation of Queen Victoria, whose elevation to become the nation's longest reigning monarch was threatened when she was targeted by a railway assassin in 1882. Therefore, when approached by my publisher to consider producing a book on 'The Great Train Robbery and Other Crimes', further research made it possible to include the high profile executions of Franz Muller and Percy Lefroy - Britain's first and second railway murderers; John Tawell - the first killer caught by the use of the railway telegraph; Frederick and Marie Manning – a murderous husband and wife team previously questioned about their involvement in train robberies and, last but not least, two audacious heists, that rank alongside the daring Great Train Robbery of 1963 – The Great Bullion Robbery of 1855, recalled in the 1978 movie 'The First Great Train Robbery' and, a somewhat overlooked earlier crime – The Great Western Railway Robbery committed in 1849.

My interest in railway crime was stimulated by the fact that the 1849 robbery was planned by a resident of Exeter, in my home county of Devon and, during my lifetime, Bruce Reynolds, the mastermind behind the 1963 train robbery, was captured in the town where I live. While on the run, using the alias Keith Miller, he became a member of the library where I work in Torquay. On the reverse side of his application for membership, the career criminal persuaded an unwitting neighbour to sign as guarantor in the belief that Britain's most wanted thief was 'a person whom books can be safely entrusted for perusal'.

Mike Holgate
Torquay
New Year's Day 2013

The 1968 Torquay Library membership application of Bruce Reynolds using the alias Keith Miller.

1

GREAT TRAIN ROBBERIES

Modern Day Highwaymen

The Great Train Robbery of 1963 was hailed as the 'crime of the century' and elevated hitherto small-time crooks, Bruce Reynolds, Charlie Wilson, Buster Edwards, Ronnie Biggs *et al* to the type of cult status and hero worship previously enjoyed by legendary bandits of the American 'Wild West'. Establishment figures were astonished and dismayed to discover that, as journalist Bernard Levin wryly observed, the British public 'regarded the robbers as folk heroes, and viewed the crime with glee, their enterprise with admiration, and their fate with sympathy'. By the late 1800s, train robberies were a frequent occurrence in America making household names of Frank and Jesse James and Butch Cassidy and the Sundance Kid. These outlaw exploits are still continually glamorised in novels and films - one of the first-ever features with a recognisable storyline - 'replete with thrilling and exciting incidents in fourteen scenes' - starred Bronco Billy Anderson in 'The Great Train Robbery' (1903). In Britain, apart from cases of organised pilfering by railway employees, raids mounted on a moving train have been extremely rare and the culprits nearly always brought to justice. However, a spate of significant

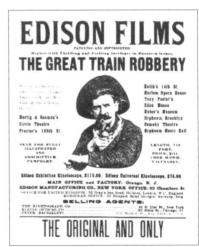

heists took place in England a quarter of a century before the James Gang plundered their first train in 1873, when a new breed of villain termed, 'The Modern Dick Turpin', replaced romanticised highwaymen and turned their attention from stagecoaches to steam trains, resulting in the theft of a fortune in gold preceding a double-robbery when a king's ransom in cash and valuables were rifled from mail sacks on the Great Western Railway.

The Great Western Railway Robberies

On New Year's Day 1849, the first of two daring robberies took place on the 6.35pm Plymouth to London mail train. The perpetrators of the crime, Henry Poole and Edward Nightingale, boarded a first-class carriage and during the journey between Exeter and Bristol gained entry to the unguarded mail van and helped themselves to property valued at over £150,000 (today worth £13million) which was disposed of and never recovered. The crooks then impudently attempted a repeat performance on the return journey. The mail sacks were found to have been tampered with at Bridgewater and following a search of the train, incriminating evidence was discovered. The pair were then arrested on suspicion and detained at Exeter. The case attracted national interest and featured a headline in the *Times*: 'Extraordinary Robbery On The Great Western Railway'.

Edward Nightingale was 'wanted' for another undisclosed crime and refused to give his name. He was not identified until the commencement of the Magistrates Hearing at Exeter Guildhall, when Detective-sergeant Edward Langley of Scotland Yard appeared in court and confirmed that the defendant was a 'horse dealer' from Hoxton, London, and well known to the police. Nightingale's father George, who had died about six months earlier, was also a villain. He had been a bookmaker at Goodwood and according to the press had 'obtained considerable notoriety by his gambling transactions'. Like his son, Nightingale senior was also a mail robber; in 1827 he was acquitted of robbing the Dover to

'Don't worry my dear, the only robbery on this journey is the price of the tickets.'

London stagecoach after producing witnesses to say that on the night of the crime he had been in the Three Tuns tavern at Tiverton, near Exeter. However, as he was leaving the Maidstone courthouse, he was arrested for another highway robbery, committed two years earlier in Warwick.

The *Illustrated London News* discovered that, 'Poole belongs to a respectable family from Taunton, but has not been on friendly terms with them since he commenced his present plundering pursuits'. Nine months before the robbery, Poole and his wife (reportedly once a lady's maid in service with the Duchess of Sutherland) had seemingly come into a fortune and, according to conflicting reports; he had either been forced to resign or was discharged from his job as a Great Western Railway guard. He took an elegant residence in Exeter with twenty 'superbly furnished' rooms and soon after his arrest instructed 'friends' to sell his valuable effects. The *Exeter Gazette* reported that special catalogues were printed and the lots attracted high bids over two whole sales days. The auctioneer remarked that the 'furniture was fit for the mansion of any nobleman'. Despite his wealthy lifestyle, further funded by lucrative money lending activities, Poole could not resist the lure of easy money and risked his liberty for a treasure trove utilising 'inside knowledge' gained while he was a guard on the mail trains. Planning had taken months and Poole had experimented with various disguises to avoid being recognised by his former railway colleagues as explained in *Trewman's Exeter Flying Post*:

> *Since his retirement from the Great Western, Poole has frequently appeared in the streets of Exeter in singular costume; in many cases most grotesquely attired; and it has been on many occasions observed that he has travelled up and down the line dressed in this style. ... Three or four months since, when dressed as a labouring man, he was found in what is technically called 'the locker' of a railway carriage (the place in which the parcels are deposited), but little or no suspicion was excited on account of the plausible excuses which the man offered for his conduct.*

A GWR train passing Dawlish near Starcross, 1850.

Donning false moustaches and unfamiliar garb - Nightingale wearing a reversible coat of contrasting colours and Poole, a cloak with a high collar and a green felt broad rimmed hat - the felons put their plan into action a few miles from Exeter at Starcross. After having a drink at the Courtenay Arms, they bought one-way tickets on the station and boarded the night train, seating themselves in one of the private compartments of the spacious broad gauge first class carriage behind the mail tender. Poole knew from experience, that while the train was travelling between Exeter and Bristol, the guard left the mail van unattended to assist the clerks in the sorting of letters on the adjoining Travelling Post Office. With no stop between Bridgewater and Bristol, there was a window of opportunity allowing the thieves a little over one hour to make their way precariously along the footboards on the outside of the train, using a hook to secure a hold on the top of the carriage, then enter the mail van and plunder the sealed bags containing registered letters and bankers parcels. The heist was a complete success and they apparently disposed of their plunder to the keeping of an unknown accomplice at Bristol, then shortly after midnight had a

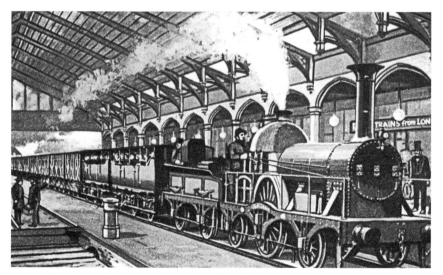

Bristol Temple Meads where the mail robbery was discovered.

The robbers were caught on the return journey from Bristol to Exeter.

celebratory drink of brandy and water in the Talbot Inn before calmly purchasing tickets for the return journey. Greed was to be their downfall; for they could have escaped unnoticed and got clean away as pandemonium ensued when the rifled bags were discovered by baffled railway staff, with no clues to help the investigation that was immediately instigated.

By coincidence, a passenger on the 'down' train from Bristol to Exeter was Superintendent Joseph Gibbons of Plymouth police. At Bridgewater, guards informed him that the mailbags had been robbed. Realising that the thieves must still be on-board the train, he ordered a search of the carriages at Taunton. Poole and Nightingale, seated suspiciously with the blinds drawn in a compartment of the first-class carriage, were quickly rumbled when a dozen packages were found under their seats wrapped in a shawl together with false moustaches, crepe masks, hook, string, candle and sealing wax. When questioned about the booty both men replied, 'We know nothing about it'. They also denied knowing each other and Nightingale attempted to bluff his way out of trouble by insisting, 'I am a respectable man and have fifty men in my employ'. As they were arrested on suspicion, under-guard John Thomas saw through the disguise of his former colleague and called out; 'That's Harry Poole'.

The thieves returned to Exeter, not as rich men, but prisoners. The key to the failure of their plan was highlighted in evidence given by Leonard Barrett, mail guard on the 'down' train. He explained that when Poole had worked for the Great Western Railway, the oil lamps of the mail van were fixed on the inside of the doorway. Recently, these had been replaced by roof lamps, which made it impossible for the felons to use the candle and wax found in their possession. It was evident that they had intended to light the candle from the lamp and melt the wax to reseal the bags and prevent all possibility of detection until the bags reached their final destination. Instead, the bags were merely re-tied with string and the theft was readily discovered on the outward journey when the train reached Bristol, not London. Without this hitch their plan would have bought them more time to plunder the 'down' train but Poole and Nightingale did not assess the risk, or merely ignored the possibility, that the railway guards had been alerted to the fact that a robbery had taken place when they reported for duty on the return train at Bristol and were bound to be extra vigilant.

Counsel for the defendants in his closing speech intimated that entry to the mail tender from the first-class carriage in the dark was far too dangerous to contemplate on a train travelling at speeds up to 50mph, arguing, 'Why a cat could not have done it.' However, the jury had already heard how intrepid mail guard Leonard Barrett had proved otherwise in a risky re-enactment: 'I have made a trial to ascertain if anyone could pass from the first-class carriage to the Post-office tender. I did so … on the down train between Bristol and Bridgewater. I proceeded from the door of the third compartment of the first-class carriage along the steps, then over the buffers of the carriage and tender, taking hold of the handles of the parcels department, on to the step of the Post-office van, and then walked along the steps and lifted the window with my nail, and then got in. I did this while the train was in motion'.

The trial, attended by leading figures from the Great Western,

Bristol & Exeter and South Devon railway companies, commenced on Friday 23 March at the Spring Assizes held at Exeter Castle. The prosecution had insufficient evidence to connect Poole and Nightingale with the 'up' train robbery, from which valuables were missing, estimated in excess of £150,000. However, the prisoners faced charges for the theft of only £150 worth of miscellaneous articles from the 'down' train including: twelve letters, six rings, a watchcase and gold ring mountings. Nevertheless, the stealing of any property belonging to HM Postmaster General could result in transportation for life. The jury took only half-an-hour to return a verdict of 'Guilty' against both prisoners. The judge, Lord Denman, commended the jury on their deliberation before addressing the accused: 'The evidence is so strong and overpowering that to have said you were not guilty would have been inviting others to commit similar crimes. What can one think when a discharged guard, who comes to Exeter with no apparent motive, meets another man with no honest calling, goes to Starcross and starts to Bristol, returns by the next train, comes and conceals himself, and tells a false story? The mere fact of your being present with all that knowledge and so conducting yourself, and the disappearance of the letters, would be strong enough to show that you two were the men, and you Poole, with your evident activity and skill, concealment, disguise and falsehood, bear the strongest evidence of guilt; you must be transported for fifteen years'.

The Bermondsey Murder

During the trial of the foiled train robbers, it became evident that the Great Western Railway had been tipped off about the criminals' intentions some months earlier by two respectable Taunton men, Eales White, proprietor of the East Reach Brewery and surgeon James Dyer. Details of a 'remarkable prophecy' were revealed by *Trewman's Exeter Flying Post*: 'We are in a position to assert an extraordinary fact connected with these Jack Sheppard-like achievements … The information was given … by the wife of one of the supposed accomplices in this and many other "railway schemes"'. The *Taunton Courier* confirmed the story:

The communication was made most circumstantially to the persons named as to the mode in which the late robbery was to be effected, and the description of the disguise to be used was minutely described, even to the 'moustaches' found in the railway carriage occupied by the prisoners. … the communication was made by the wife of the man said to be implicated in the robbery while in a paroxysm of anger arising from the ill-usage she had experienced. He had, consistently with his accustomed brutality, turned her out of his house, and it was while she was consulting those to whom she had appealed for advice that the various and long-continued enormities of her husband had been disclosed.

The woman who revealed the secret of the conspiracy was Maria Manning, the vexed wife of Frederick Manning, landlord of the White Hart Inn, Taunton, where the train robbery had been planned. It was no coincidence that the publican's closest friend was Henry Poole. Before entering the licensed trade, Manning had also been employed as a Great Western Railway guard and had first

Frederick Manning.

met lady's maid Maria when she regularly accompanied her mistress Lady Palk on the London train from Exeter, where her ladyship resided on the outskirts of the city at Haldon House. Although there was not enough evidence upon which to proceed with a prosecution, Manning was apparently dismissed by the Great Western Railway when suspected of being involved in a spate of thefts culminating in the mysterious disappearance of gold valued at £5,000 (now worth £425,000) on 10 January 1848. It appears that both Poole and Manning may have parted company with the Great Western Railway following an internal investigation into this affair when the *Times* announced developments at Taunton: 'Several of the company's servants from the station where the suspected persons alighted were brought up and examined, and it is said that circumstances have transpired that will eventually lead to the apprehension of the parties implicated in the robbery'. The bullion box had been loaded at Paddington bound for Taunton, but when a superintendent at Bristol inspected it, the entire contents had been removed by gaining entry to the box 'dextrously cut by means of a circular saw, or similar instrument, and the work was that of some practiced hands'. The carriage adjoining that 'in which the treasure was deposited', was occupied by 'six persons of fashionable appearance', whom the police believed were criminals belonging to the London 'swell mob' of which, it later transpired, Edward Nightingale was a prominent member. This particular crime may have been the one for which the villain was sought by the police and the reason why he refused to confirm his name until identified by a detective at Exeter Assizes in 1849.

If Edward Manning was the 'third man' to whom Poole and Nightingale handed the £150,000 haul from the Great Western Robbery, he clearly profited little from the proceeds. The *Manchester Times* revealed that the felons would be unable to cash in their ill-gotten gains: :

It is understood, upon the best authority, from an inspection of the returns of the various local postmasters and the invoices at the head office, that although the actual property contained in the 'up' train was immense, the amount in reality realisable by the robbers will not exceed £200, since it consisted chiefly of bills of exchange, securities and bank notes, the numbers and descriptions of which ... were instantly telegraphed to the parties and stopped.

Fortunate to be released after facing police questioning about their role in the latest train robbery, Frederick and Maria Manning, who had incurred debts and lost the White Hart Inn during their marriage wrangles, moved to London and settled in Bermondsey. They rented a house at Miniver Place, which, they planned to share with a previous suitor of Maria's called Patrick O'Connor. According to author

Maria Manning.

Robert Huish who published a series of broadsides recording *The Authentic Memoirs of Maria Manning,* in 1849, they had met seven years earlier when Maria (born Marie de Roux, at Geneva in 1821) was working at an inn where she met Patrick when he was in service with an Irish family named Wentworth who were holidaying in Switzerland. Although more than twice her age, Patrick was immediately smitten with the girl and persuaded his employers that she would be suitable for the position of lady's maid. Therefore, Maria returned to the couple's mansion of Ballincraig in County Kilkenny, where her affair with Patrick ended suddenly when Mr Wentworth caught the lovers locked in a passionate embrace and dismissed the aggrieved O'Connor. Further scandal ensued when Mrs Wentworth's suspicions were also aroused and upon 'opening the door of the library in the softest manner', discovered 'her beloved and continent husband sitting on the sofa with her chaste and immaculate servant affectionately seated on his knee'. The outraged Mrs Wentworth flew at the shamed girl and scratched her face before ordering the 'vicious, abominable hussy' from her household. Maria's next position ended with the premature death of Lady Palk in January 1846. With glowing references from her ladyship's widowed husband, Devonshire landowner and Member of Parliament, Sir Lawence Palk, she moved to London as a lady's maid to Lady Ballantyre, the daughter of the Duke and Duchess of Sutherland, at the majestic Stafford House, near Buckingham Palace. Later that year she renewed her acquaintance with Patrick O'Connor whilst travelling across the Channel to Boulogne to join her new mistress. Her forty-eight year-old former lover from Tipperary, had come up in the world and was

Patrick O'Connor.

taking a break from his job as a customs officer in the London Docks. This was an ironic profession for someone who regularly abused his position with smuggling activities of his own, whilst also dabbling in fraud by demanding payment to help job seekers find employment in the docks. O'Connor also built up a lucrative money-lending venture among his work colleagues and invested the profits in foreign railway stocks.

Both O'Connor and Manning wanted to marry Maria, but she chose the latter, swayed by news of a £400 inheritance received following the death of his father, a former sergeant in the Somerset militia, who later ran The Bear public house in Taunton. A stylish wedding was arranged and took place at St James Church, Piccadilly in June 1847. When O'Connor learned of the marriage he was devastated and wrote an anguished letter to Stafford House: 'Ah, Maria! You have acted cruelly to me. Why not, like a true professor of what you avowed, write and say what you intended before you acted so, then, at the risk of losing my situation, I would have gone every step that man could, and got married to the only being on the face of the earth who could make me happy'.

Frederick Manning was soon to rue winning Maria's hand. His choice of bride did not altogether impress members of his family and the groom belatedly admitted to his brother Edmund, 'I should never have married that woman if I had listened to your advice'. Following the Great Western Railway guard's dismissal from his job, the marriage foundered and after informing on the train robbery plotters, Maria took the White Hart's takings and fled to revive her affair with O'Connor in London. Later reconciled with Manning, who, if involved in the Great Western Railway robbery had clearly not profited greatly from it, the pair had no visible means of support and they conspired to kill O'Connor and relieve him of his considerable wealth. The two men appeared to be on good terms despite their rivalry for Maria's affection. Frederick even offered to let Patrick move in at Miniver Place to share the rent (and possibly Maria in a ménage a trios). O'Connor reneged on the agreement causing the Mannings to temporarily take in a medical student as a lodger. Maria easily manipulated the two men in her life and she appears to have taken the lead in the murder plot. The foul deed was committed on Thursday 9 August 1849, when O'Connor accepted an invitation to dine at Miniver Place. The couple purchased implements in preparation for the crime; Frederick bought a pistol and a crowbar, while Maria obtained a shovel and took delivery of some quicklime. A hole was dug beneath flagstones in the basement kitchen, in which to bury the body. After leaving work at the docks, O'Connor walked unsuspectingly to his death at Miniver Place. When he arrived for dinner, Maria led him to the kitchen past the hole, which she said had been excavated for work on the drains. As her guest washed his hands and face in the sink, she coldly produced a pistol and shot him in the back of the head. O'Connor still showed signs of life so Frederick then finished him off with seventeen blows to the head delivered with the crowbar. The victim was then stripped of his clothes before his arms and legs were bent back and trussed to the trunk with rope. The corpse was then dropped face down into the pit, treated with quicklime to eat the body away, before the flagstones were replaced and re-plastered with cement to conceal all trace of wrong-doing. The couple then calmly sat down to dine and heartily ate the goose that Maria had ostensibly cooked for three people.

Maria Manning had been a frequent visitor to O'Connor's lodgings over a shop in Mile End. The landlady had been instructed by her tenant to allow Maria to enter his rooms at any time. Armed with a key to a cashbox removed from the dead man's pocket, Maria wasted no time to collect the valuables that had made O'Connor such a good marriage prospect. She quickly helped herself to £4,000 in cash, share certificates and foreign railway stocks. Two days later, Frederick impersonated O'Connor to trade some shares and called in at a bank to obtain change for a £100 note. Meanwhile, O'Connor's colleagues reported him missing when he did not turn up for work and the police made enquiries at Miniver Place. The Mannings denied any knowledge of their friend's whereabouts and claimed that their guest must have changed his mind for he had not arrived at the arranged time. However, when the police called again, the murderers panicked and fled their home on Monday 13 August. That same day, a cousin of O'Connor's, William Flynn, visited the moneylender's rooms and discovered that his cashbox had been looted. Hurrying round to Miniver Place he learned that Maria had left in a hansom cab with several large trunks. The following day, second-hand dealer Charles Bainbridge, who had paid Frederick Manning £13 for the furniture, emptied the house. The police did

The body of the murder victim is discovered.

not suspect foul play until a thorough search of the house was conducted on Friday 17 August. Two police officers noticed the extra tidiness of the kitchen and the fresh cement on the floor. They called in some workmen to lift the flagstones and made the gruesome discovery of O'Connor's decomposed body.

A hue and cry ensued. The hunt was now on for the perpetrators of the crime. A watch was put on ports, as it was believed that Maria would attempt to return to mainland Europe, but she had travelled in a first class train carriage to Edinburgh. She was apprehended in the Scottish capital after arousing suspicion by trying to sell the foreign railway stocks she had stolen from O'Connor. A stockbroker noted the address of her hotel and informed the police of her whereabouts. When she was arrested, her baggage was searched revealing cash totalling £188. Her foreign accent had given away her identity to the stockbroker who was alerted because she foolishly tried to pass herself off as the daughter of a Glaswegian

The police hunt for Maria Manning ended at the Edinburgh hotel.

named Robertson. More than a third of the money in her possession was savings accrued by her husband Frederick who had been left penniless and abandoned to his fate by his scheming spouse. With only the proceeds of the furniture, he journeyed on the train from Waterloo to Southampton and took the midnight ferry to Jersey. Staying at a hotel in St Helier, he tried to pass himself off as a gin salesman, but his favourite tipple proved to be brandy and his heavy drinking and vulgar behaviour attracted unwanted attention. When he saw a man he recognised from his hometown of Taunton, Frederick left St Helier, wisely deciding to keep a low profile by renting rooms in a property in the country called Prospect Cottage. The rent was four shillings (20p) a week, although his money was rapidly diminishing as he continually downed alcohol, doubtless in an effort to wipe out the memory of the brutal death of his love rival and the subsequent betrayal by his duplicitous wife. Alerted to the fugitive's presence on the island, Detective-sergeant Edward Langley, who had previously identified Edward Nightingale for the criminal court and interviewed the Mannings to ascertain what they knew about the Great Western Railway robberies, travelled to Jersey accompanied by another officer from Scotland Yard. On Monday 27 August, after two and a half weeks at large, Manning was roused from his sleep and arrested as he lay in bed. His immediate reaction was to enquire, 'Is the wretch taken?' When the police officers confirmed that Maria was in custody, he commented, 'Thank God: I am glad of it; that will save my life. She is the guilty party; I am as innocent as a lamb'. Although later acknowledging that he dealt the final deathblow, Manning continued to protest his innocence; despite his admission that he had repeatedly smashed the victim's skull with a crowbar he bizarrely told his brother Edmund 'I never hurt a hair of his head'.

The 'Bermondsey Murder' had attracted blanket coverage in the newspapers and the trial was eagerly awaited by the British public. The proceedings opened at the Old Bailey on Thursday 25 October and lasted two days. The prisoners did not help their cause by attempting to accuse each other for O'Connor's death. In his summing up, defence counsel for the husband conceded that he was to adopt a line that was 'odious' but he hoped to convince the jury that in this case a woman had made her husband a 'dupe' and now sought to save herself by his destruction. She was wicked and quite capable of murder. Defence counsel for Maria condemned his learned friend for the way his client had tried to blacken the name of a woman and in reply attempted to demonstrate that having been ill-treated by her husband, she had turned to her long-time admirer O'Connor, and was not likely to murder someone for property she could easily have obtained by 'other means'.

The jury retired and within forty-five minutes had no difficulty in returning a verdict of 'Guilty against both prisoners'. When asked if there was anything the prisoners would like to say before sentence was pronounced, Frederick declined leaving centre stage to Maria who accepted the opportunity to make an impassioned plea from the dock: 'Mr O'Connor was more to me than my husband. He wanted to marry me, and I ought to have been married to him. I have letters which would prove his respect and regard; and I think, considering that I am a woman and alone, that I have to fight against my husband's statements, that I have to fight against the prosecutors, and that even the Judge is against me - I think that I am not treated like a Christian, but like a wild beast of the forest'.

Unimpressed by this tirade, Mr Justice Cresswell, proceeded to don the black cap and summarily pass sentence of death commenting: 'Murder is at all times a horrible offence, but the present murder is one of the most cold-blooded and deliberately calculated I ever remember. It is one of the most appalling instances of human wickedness which the annals of this court can furnish'.

Once in the condemned cells, the warring couple continued to blame each other for their plight. In a letter to Frederick, Maria refused his requests for a meeting until he agreed to state in writing that she was innocent suggesting a plot from her fertile imagination, 'You know that the young man from Jersey who was smoking in the back parlour committed the murder, and that I was from home when it was committed'. In retaliation, Frederick made allegations about Maria reported in the *Times*. 'The miserable man perseveres in his assertion that his wife committed the murder, and threatened to take his life also unless he became her accomplice'. While the culprits were on the run the same newspaper revealed that Manning was 'a discharged railway servant, who was dismissed by the directors of the Great Western Railway Company some time ago for being concerned with Nightingale and others in committing a series of robberies on that line'. With the prisoner facing the death penalty it became clear that the prisoner was prepared to make some disclosures 'with reference to some robberies in which he has been concerned' to form the basis of an application 'to grant him a respite'.

The Home Secretary dismissed the appeals from the bickering Mannings. Reconciled to their fate they tenderly kissed and made up in the chapel on the day they were to face their final judgement. Hangman William Calcraft was chosen to officiate at the first execution of a husband and wife since 1700. Charles Dickens witnessed his handiwork at the public execution at Horsemonger Lane Gaol. A supporter of capital punishment although bitterly opposed to public executions, the distinguished writer was one of London's fashionable set who had paid up to ten guineas to rent houses offering a good view of the scaffold. This class of people were nothing more than obscene voyeurs with ladies using opera glasses as they would if attending a play on the London stage; yet, the author with a social conscience, who was to use Maria Manning as the basis for the character of murderess Mademoiselle Hortense in his classic novel *Bleak House*, directed his disgust at the carnival atmosphere amongst the poor 'ruffians and vagabonds' clearly enjoying the rare treat of a double hanging. The event was attended by an immense crowd of 50,000, attracting street hawkers and entertainers, pickpockets and prostitutes, all plying their trade, while people waited patiently for the main attraction, passing the time by reading souvenirs commemorating the crime and singing parodies of 'negro melodies', for example, substituting the phrase 'Oh Mrs Manning' for 'Oh Susannah'. The execution took place at 9am on Tuesday 13 November but the festivities outside the prison had commenced the previous evening. Dickens arrived upon the scene at midnight and observed in a letter to the *Times*:

When the sun rose brightly - as it did - it gilded the faces of thousands upon thousands of upturned faces, so inexpressively odious in their brutal mirth of callousness, that a man had cause to feel ashamed of the shape he wore, and to shrink from himself, as fashioned in the image of the Devil. When the two miserable creatures who attracted

Execution of the Mannings.

*all this ghastly sight about them were turned quivering into the air,
there was no more emotion, no more pity, no more thought that two
immortal souls had gone to judgement, no more restraint in any of the
previous obscenities, than if the name of Christ had never been heard
in the world.*

Earlier that year, the Mannings had avoided arrest after being interrogated by the police about their knowledge of the Great Western Railway robberies, but their relief had been short-lived as justice finally caught up with them over far more serious charges. When the death penalty was carried out on Frederick Manning, Henry Poole was enduring the rigours of convict life in Australia and could not conduct his duties as co-executor of his friend's will, while the chief beneficiary, Maria Manning, was in no position to receive her pitiful bequest. The whole sorry affair was summed up with an unintended railway pun contained in the second line of a verse from a poem published on a popular broadsheet entitled *The Bermondsey Tragedy*:

> *The end of poor O'Connor will long in memory reign,*
> *And shew the vice and folly which followed in its train.*
> *Oh! may it thus a warning prove to shun bad company;*
> *Never like the Mannings commit such a tragedy.*

The Great Bullion Robbery

Edward Manning and his fellow railway guard Henry Poole had both been dismissed by the Great Western Railway following the theft of gold sovereigns from a strongbox on the London to Bristol train in January 1848. The valuables were never recovered, a feat that inspired William Pierce, a disgruntled railway employee dismissed for the suspected petty theft of railway tickets, to dream of stealing a gold shipment carried by the object of his antipathy - the South Eastern Railway Company. In 1850, the former ticket printer, turned grocer, first discussed the possibility of committing the bold crime with professional criminal and expert locksmith Edward Agar (also known as Archer and Adams but whose real name was Roberts). Pierce persisted with the idea for a further five years before finally convincing his doubting accomplice that the ingenious plan was really viable. With the recruitment of station clerk William Tester and rail guard James Burgess, the meticulous operation was brilliantly executed, baffling police forces on both sides of the English Channel. The thieves successfully targeted a train carrying gold bullion from London to Folkestone and from Boulogne to Paris in May 1855. *Lloyds Weekly News* carried a sensational account of the crime with a banner   headline pronouncing 'The Great Bullion Robbery':

> *An extensive robbery of bullion has been committed on the way from London to Paris, evidently perpetrated by persons acquainted with the extent and mode of the consignment. Gold in bars and American coins, amounting to between £13,000–£14,000, had been deposited in three boxes, which were separately consigned to Paris, from the bullion-brokers, Thomas, Bult, and Spielman; and were taken in the mail train of the South Eastern Railway, which set off at half-past 8 o'clock on the evening of Tuesday, the 15th instant, to Folkestone, whence they were to be taken via Boulogne and the Northern Railway of France to Paris. It was found that the three boxes, which were, when delivered in London, hooped and sealed, had been reopened and plundered, and then re-hooped and resealed. It is rather remarkable that the depredators left in one of the boxes between £6,000 and £7,000 worth of gold; but it is conjectured because they had not materials at command to supply what might have been the deficiency in weight. They had filled up that box with sporting shot and the other two boxes were supplied with a quantity of shot sufficient to represent in weight the amount of gold abstracted from them. It is supposed that so well planned a scheme could not have been executed in the rapid passage from London to Folkestone.*

The press and the police supposed wrong - for the robbery had indeed taken place *en route* to Folkestone, however, an important clue was overlooked by the authorities. The boxes had been weighed and sealed at the carriers' offices in London, placed in travelling safes, then weighed again when landed by cross-channel steamer at Boulogne.

Although, the metal hoops and seals were intact, one of the gold chests was forty pounds lighter, yet, despite this discrepancy the contents of the boxes were not checked until the consignment reached Paris. Furthermore, while the English and French police were squabbling about exactly where the robbery had taken place, for months they ignored vital evidence that lead shot had been switched for gold long before reaching France. Hundreds of suspects were then questioned without result and a break-

A train passing through Bletchingley Tunnel between and Redhill and Folkestone.

through in the case only came about through a confession by one of the perpetrators, Edward Agar. The career criminal broke his silence while awaiting transportation for life after being found guilty of passing a forged cheque for £700 in August 1855. Ironically, Agar claimed he had been 'framed' by the man who set up his arrest for the crime named James Humphries, a former lover of Fanny Kay, a young woman who for the past two years had lived with Agar and borne him a child. Grudgingly accepting his fate, Agar prepared to sail to Australia on a prison hulk from Portland, believing he had left Fanny and his child well provided for. He entrusted William Pierce with £2,500, accumulated from his criminal activities, to invest on behalf of his family from which a weekly allowance would be payable to Fanny. Unfortunately, for all concerned, Agar's partner-in-crime reneged on the deal. Initially, Fanny was financed well enough to rent a comfortable house with a servant, before Pierce abandoned her and the baby who were then forced, through lack of funds, to take lodgings and share a single room with another female.

Left destitute, Fanny went to Pierce's fashionable house in Kilburn and demanded some money from the felon. An argument ensued and she was assaulted for her trouble before being sent on her way - penniless. Fanny retaliated by informing the authorities what little she knew about the bullion robbery - making sure she implicated William Pierce. When the prison governor relayed the plight of Fanny Kay to Edward Agar, the angry convict took his revenge by turning on the gang who had seemingly committed the perfect crime. In a statement to the police, he revealed exactly how the heist had been perpetrated and the names of all those involved: William Pierce (with whom he had planned the robbery); James Burgess (the railway guard who had introduced Agar to former station refreshment room waitress Fanny Kay); William Tester (the London Bridge station clerk who had now obtained a position as a railway superintendent in Switzerland), and, last but not least, James Townsend Saward, a crooked barrister who had disposed of some of the gold. Known as 'Jim the Penman' to the criminal underworld, Saward was also the brains behind an organised scheme to forge signatures on stolen cheques which had led to the demise of Edward Agar. The police suspected that Saward had employed Agar to travel to New York on several occasions to dispose of large quantities of banknotes (obtained with forged cheques) whose serial numbers were known, thereby, making it too dangerous to try and pass them in England. When questioned, Agar refused to elaborate on his trans-Atlantic trips, simply explaining that he was involved in 'speculation'. It is not beyond the bounds of possibility that the currency and securities missing from the 1849 train robbery and passed by Frederick Manning to the 'swell mob' were disposed of in the same way across the Atlantic.

London Bridge railway station.

Soon after returning from one of these trips to America in the Autumn of 1853, Agar was in London where by chance he met up with William Pierce, who was eager to reopen their earlier discussions about plans to rob a mail train. By May 1854, Agar was persuaded to explore the possibility. Pierce had recruited useful allies in William Tester, then station master at Margate who, fortuitously for the criminals was promoted and transferred to the superintendent's office at London Bridge station, and James Burgess, a long-serving guard on the mail train. In order to carry out the robbery the gang faced a formidable challenge. The main stumbling block lay in gaining access to the safes which held the bullion chests and were secured with two locks. Apart from one set entrusted to the captain of the cross channel ferry, the key to one lock was held at London Bridge station and the other at Folkestone. Fate played a hand when the London key was lost and William Tester given the responsibility of ordering a replacement from Chubb the well-known locksmith company. Tester had the new key in his possession for a limited period and took the opportunity to arrange a meeting and pass it to Agar who made a wax impression. Attention was then focused on obtaining a similar impression of the second key at Folkestone. Agar and Pierce travelled to the resort on a number of occasions posing as commercial travellers and observed the procedure surrounding the arrival and departure of bullion boxes carefully. They also visited public houses and befriended railway staff and engaged them in conversation to stealthily elicit useful information over a drink of beer or a game of billiards. Discovering that the key, vital to their plans, was kept in a cupboard in the railway office, they simply waited for the staff to leave it unattended and unlocked. When the opportunity presented itself, Agar wasted no time to enter the vacant office and swiftly obtained a wax impression while Pierce stood outside and acted as lookout. This seemingly impossible task accomplished, Agar used his considerable skill to make duplicates. He then arranged to travel several times in the guard's van from London to Folkestone, when Burgess was on duty, in order to test the keys and finalise the plan. The thieves then purchased two hundredweight of lead shot which they calculated would enable them to switch it with gold worth £12,000 (now equivalent to about £1M). The shot was placed in four carpet bags and carried by cab to London Bridge station in readiness on six separate occasions before they saw Burgess wiping his face with a handkerchief. At last, this was the signal that gold bullion was on the train and their patient plan could at last be put into action. Buying a pair of tickets to Dover, Pierce, heavily disguised in a broad-brimmed hat, black wig and whiskers to avoid recognition by former railway colleagues, travelled in a first class carriage, while Agar stealthily jumped unobserved into the guard van with Burgess. Using the keys he had fashioned, Agar opened the two safes and removed the wooden boxes. Utilising a pair of pliers to ease off the metal hoops, gold bars and coins were removed and

Station clerk William Tester.

placed in the carpet bags. Then the packets of lead shot were laid in the chests that had their iron hoops replaced before they were carefully resealed with wax. One carpet bag full of gold was passed to William Tester, who had been waiting at Redhill station, where he received the loot and boarded the next train back to London. Pierce then joined Agar and Burgess exchanging lead for gold in a race against time until they reached Folkestone. Without arousing undue suspicion, the safes were removed from the train, overseen by James Burgess, then transferred to the bullion boat waiting in the harbour bound for Boulogne. The jubilant crooks journeyed on to Dover, where Agar and Pierce enjoyed a celebratory supper at the Castle Hotel. Clutching their carpet bags, they nervously allowed an eager-to-please railway porter to carry the heavy load before nonchalantly returning to London on a train with Burgess still acting as the guard. At Agar's home, a fire-brick furnace was constructed and the gold melted down in a crucible before being passed to intermediaries, including James Townsend Saward, who were paid a commission to sell off the stolen gold. When the four thieves split the initial proceeds, Agar, Pierce and Tester received £600 while Burgess was awarded slightly more with £700. The unsolved robbery had become something of a dim memory in the

Train guard James Burgess.

public consciousness when Edward Agar made his sensational revelations and brought his fellow conspirators to trial where the prosecuting counsel observed in his opening remarks: 'It is really lamentable to reflect upon the amount of skill, dexterity, perseverance and ability exercised upon the execution of a criminal design, which this robbery displays'.

The case against James Townsend Saward and an accomplice named James Anderson, was dealt with separately and they were subsequently 'transported beyond the seas for life' to Australia on charges of issuing stolen forged cheques with intent to defraud, whilst in January 1857, the three-day trial of William Pierce, James Burgess and William Tester, charged with the theft of gold weighing 200 pounds with a worth of £12.000, came to a conclusion when the jury retired, then, after an absence of barely ten minutes, returned verdicts of 'guilty' on the three prisoners at the bar. Trial judge, Baron Martin, satisfied that the verdicts had been reached on the 'clearest evidence' passed sentences of fourteen years transportation on Burgess and Tester who had betrayed the trust of their employer. Despite the fact that, in the judge's opinion, William Pierce was 'far worse than any of the others', he regretfully pronounced that he could only gaol the instigator of the robbery for the maximum term allowed in his case, which was two years hard labour. This anomaly came about because the prisoner faced a charge of simple 'larceny' as he was no longer in the service of the railway company. To cheers from the public gallery, the judge denounced Pierce for his treatment of that 'wretched woman - call her harlot if you will' Fanny Kay, whom he had 'mercilessly robbed' making him 'the greatest villain in the world'. Although only £2,000 of the £12,000 worth of gold had been recovered, at Baron Martin's

Edward Agar.

recommendation, Fanny Kay was subsequently awarded the sum of £2,500 to be placed in a trust fund for her and her child. This was the amount deducted from Edward Agar's 'savings' that William Pierce had invested in Turkish bonds for his own benefit. As Edward Agar had not been tried in connection with the robbery, it was ruled that the prosecution had no right to seize the funds. Speaking of the chief witness for the Crown, whose role in the affair the judge believed had been 'romanticised' - budding wrongdoers were warned of the dangers of misplaced admiration for the criminal activities of Agar:

He is a man of extraordinary talent. No doubt he has given to the details of this robbery a great deal of thought. If he had devoted one tenth of his ability on any honest pursuit, it must have raised him to a respectable station in life, that would probably have enabled him to realise a large fortune. However, instead of being a man of respectability, he is a slave for life - separated from everything that is dear to him, even the other sex, to which he is evidently attached. He is the most unenviable slave that ever trod the face of the earth and has no control over his destiny.

Baron Martin's theme about the lost opportunities of forty-one-year-old Edward Agar's wasted life was developed in a summary of the case published in the *Morning Post*:

Agar, a man with a cool head, a clear and firm hand, a resolute will, full of intelligence, a mechanician, a carpenter, a metallist, a lock and white smith, a jeweller, a turner in wood, adroit and skilful in every respect, and with a good account at his banker's - possessing as he did £3,000 stock and £700 in Spanish Bonds - was applied to by the supremer scoundrel, Pierce, because of his great professional skill, to enter into the scheme of gold robbery; and at first he deemed the scheme hazardous, if not wholly impracticable, unless a certain key could be obtained. When it was made manifest to him that this was possible and practicable, he entered into the speculation with all his heart and soul, with all his strength and intelligence, and, after twelve months of essaying and toiling, at length succeeded in robbing £12,000. The patient toil, the wariness, the pausing, balancing, yet determined skill with which the robbery was effected was a wonder of crime and well as of craft and circumspection. Half the skill, half the energy, half the perseverance of this intelligent robber, directed in an honest course, would have long made his fortune. But like many men with a tithe of his ability, he wished to be rich, and rich suddenly, without patient labour or industry; and the result is, that though he clutched much of what, in the vocabulary of the craftsman's art, is called 'swag', he lost all, even liberty itself, in his last desperate venture. His tempter and accomplice, Pierce, proved a perfidious friend, a violator of a sacred trust, and broke 'honour amongst thieves' in not giving to the mistress of Agar, Fanny Kay, the money intended for her and her innocent child. Had it not been for this breach of trust the perpetrators of the robbery, notwithstanding all our science, civilisation and skill, might have gone undiscovered and unpunished. Agar, however, notwithstanding all his crimes and villanies, had a touch of a better nature - had in a word, a heart. When under sentence for another crime, he learned how Pierce had broken faith with Fanny Kay, the mother of his child, and resolved from that moment to reveal all he knew. To this circumstance is owed the discovery of the perpetrators of the crime and their conviction.

Contemplating his long exile in Australia, Baron Martin's words about enforced 'slavery' came back to haunt Edward Agar. Despite the fact he had 'informed' on his co-conspirators, it was reported that a newly arrived convict assured him that his name was a legend amongst the criminal fraternity back home. The chastened forger, locksmith and train robber, still yearning for his common law wife and child, glumly replied, 'That means nothing, nothing at all'.

The Great Train Robbery

Novelist Michael Crichton produced a fictionalised account of the 1855 bullion heist in *The Great Train Robbery* which, when adapted into a movie starring Sean Connery as William Pierce, Donald Sutherland as Edward Agar and Michael Elphick as James Burgess, was renamed *The First Great Train Robbery* (1978). The change of title was made to distinguish it from a similar crime that was still fresh in the minds of cinema-goers - the infamous Great Train Robbery of 1963.

The more recent train robbery was the proudest moment in the crooked life of Bruce Reynolds, the mastermind of the operation nicknamed 'Napoleon'. The achievement so impressed the students of Southampton University that they elected him a honorary life member of their union. Long before his involvement in the infamous train robbery, Reynolds had a string of convictions for larceny, receiving, housebreaking, assault and causing grievous bodily harm. In 1962, his gang was suspected of taking part in a daring daylight robbery at Heathrow Airport, stealing a payroll protected by an armoured car which, netted the gang £62,000, before the same 'firm' joined forces with one led by Thomas Wisbey and set its sights much higher for the next job when Bruce Reynolds, meticulously devised a plan to hit the Glasgow to London night train carrying £2.5M (today worth £40M) in used untraceable banknotes, that were on their way to be destroyed at the Royal Mint. Around 3am on 8 August, the train was cleverly brought to a halt by rigging a railway signal located on an isolated stretch of track at Cheddington, near Leighton Buzzard. Driver Jack Mills obeyed the signal and stopped the locomotive allowing fireman David Whitby to step down from the cab. He attempted to make a call to the signal box from a trackside telephone only to find that the wires had been cut. Returning to the engine, he and the driver were confronted by Buster Edwards and Bob Welch, while Roy James swiftly uncoupled the coaches. Ronnie Biggs had brought along a former train driver to take control of the train, but he was nervous and seemed to be taking too long, cautiously waiting for the correct steam pressure to

Scene of the Great Train Robbery.

build up in the locomotive. Although James Hussey confessed on his deathbed in 2012, that he attacked the driver, it is generally believed that Buster Edwards needlessly coshed Jack Mills over the head for initially refusing to move the train along the track to where the thieves had parked stolen getaway vehicles. Once, this manoeuvre had been completed by the semi-concussed driver, a human chain was formed to load 150 moneybags onto an old army truck. There was a service base nearby, so most of the robbers wore army uniforms to avoid suspicion. The loot was then transported thirty miles to a rented farmhouse.

Like a scene from a vintage Ealing comedy, or the subsequent spoof movie *The Great St Trinian's Train Robbery* (1965), the jubilant crooks counted their ill-gotten gains and passed the time by playing Monopoly with stolen banknotes - carelessly leaving their fingerprints on the board. However, the hold-up gang had ordered the staff on the train not to give the alarm for thirty minutes which alerted the police to concentrate their search in a close vicinity of the crime. Villains enlisted to remove incriminating evidence from the farmhouse lost their nerve when they realised the police were closing in and did not carry out their allotted task. When the police, led by Jack Slipper of Scotland Yard's Flying Squad, located the gang's hideout at Leatherslade Farm, they found an embarrassment of clues and made short work of rounding up the majority of the culprits. Savage sentences were handed out at the

Buster Edwards.

conclusion of the trials of the train robbers in 1964, with seven of them, Ronnie Biggs, Gordon Goody, Robert Welch, Thomas Wisbey, James Hussey, Charley Wilson and Roy James receiving concurrent terms of twenty-five years for conspiracy to rob the mail and thirty years for armed robbery - despite the fact that no firearms had been used. A slightly more lenient sentence of twenty years was handed

Charley Wilson.

out to Roger Cordrey, the only participant to admit his guilt. Brian and Leonard Field (not related) each received a twenty-five year jail term reduced upon appeal to five years. John Wheater, a bent solicitor, served three years, while, perhaps the unluckiest defendant of all was Bill Boal He was arrested with Roger Cordrey and caught in possession of £141,000. Gang leader, Bruce Reynolds later insisted that he had never heard of Boal and claimed the. police had arrested an 'innocent man' who was not involved in the robbery.

Ronnie Biggs.

However, Boal was charged with receiving stolen goods and jailed for twenty-four years, later reduced to fourteen on appeal, although, he never regained his freedom, dying of cancer in jail in 1970. With £2million of the stolen money still missing, sentences of over 300 years were passed on the perpetrators, although, on average they spent only ten years in prison before being released in the 1970s.

The Great Train Robbery remained hot news with high profile gang members Bruce Reynolds, Jimmy White and Buster Edwards remaining on the run and sensational prison escapes by Charley Wilson in 1964 and Ronnie Biggs in 1965. Former paratrooper, Jimmy White, described as the gang's 'quartermaster' was apprehended in Kent in 1966, sentenced to eighteen years imprisonment then released nine years later in 1975.

Ronald 'Buster' Edwards, accompanied by his wife June escaped to Mexico, joining Bruce Reynolds and his family, but the couple became homesick and returned to England. Edwards surrendered voluntarily in 1966, but any hopes of a light sentence were dashed when he received fifteen years for robbery and twelve years for conspiracy.

Following his early release in 1975, Edwards went back to his old trade as a flower seller outside Waterloo Station in London. In 1988, his story was filmed starring rock star Phil Collins in the title role *Buster*, before his life ended tragically at the age of 63 in 1994, when he died after drinking heavily. His body was discovered hanging from a steel girder in a lock-up garage in Lambeth. Although a coroner's inquest recorded an open verdict, there was speculation that the fear of returning to prison, as he was under investigation by the police for large-scale fraud, may have prompted him to commit suicide. As a mark of respect for his criminal prowess, two wreaths in the shape of trains accompanied his funeral cortege.

Charley Wilson was the gang's 'treasurer' responsible for distributing the stolen money and giving each of the robbers their cut of the haul. He was captured quickly and jailed for 30 years. During the trial at Aylesbury Crown Court in 1964 he got the nickname 'the silent man' for refusing to say anything at all about the crime. He was jailed for thirty years but escaped after just four months. He was freed by a gang of three men who broke into Winston Green maximum security prison during the

Bruce Reynolds.

early hours of the morning. Having stolen a ladder from a nearby builders' yard to break into the grounds of a mental hospital next to the prison, the intruders used a rope ladder to scale the prison wall. They then coshed one of the two patrolling warders on duty and tied him up before opening Wilson's cell door with a key apparently obtained from an 'inside' source. The wanted man was recaptured in Canada after four years on the run, then extradited back to Britain where he spent a period of ten years in jail. With the exception of Ronnie Biggs, Wilson was the final train robber to emerge from prison in 1978. He later became embroiled in the vicious aftermath of the infamous Brinks-Mat gold bullion robbery committed in 1993. Vying with 'The Great Train Robbery' as the 'crime of the century', a gang of six thugs made off with £26M in gold, diamonds and cash held at the Brinks-Mat warehouse at Heathrow Airport. Terrified staff had petrol poured over them and were threatened with a lit match until they revealed the combination numbers of the vault. One of the robbers, Micky McAvoy, and his brother-in-law, security guard insider Anthony Black, were caught and imprisoned, but the loot was not recovered and became the subject of gang warfare as efforts were made to reinvest it in other criminal activity, notably the drug trade. Charlie Wilson, who had moved to Marbella, found himself in trouble with so-called 'investors' when £3million of Brinks-Mat villains money went missing in such a drug deal. He paid the ultimate price when he and his pet dog were shot and killed, as they sat by the swimming pool of his hacienda, by a young hit-man wearing a 'hoodie' who coolly escaped from the scene of the crime by riding away on a bicycle in 1990.

Ronnie Biggs cunningly adopted an interesting defence when he claimed he had been recruited only to 'clean-up' the robbers hideout at Leatherslade Farm. The jury failed to agree but at a re-trial he was found guilty and received the same harsh punishment as his fellow conspirators. A carpenter by trade and a thief by inclination, Biggs had befriended Bruce Reynolds while the pair were in jail. He became the most infamous of the train robbers when he scaled the wall of Wandsworth Prison and leapt onto the top of a waiting furniture van in July 1965. Collecting his hidden share of the train robbery money, Biggs fled to France, then Australia, with his wife and family and, finally, Brazil where he became a celebrity after he avoided extradition due to the fact that his local girlfriend Raimunda de Castro, was expecting their child, Michael. The death, in a road accident in 1970, of his ten-tear-old son Nicholas, the eldest of three children by his wife Charmian, who had remained in Australia, did not succeed in luring the grief-stricken fugitive from his South American lair. Nor did a failed kidnap attempt by ex-army officers in 1981. Fortunately, for Biggs, the boat on which he was held against his will experienced mechanical problems in the West Indies. The stranded kidnappers, who hoped to receive a reward for returning their captive to Britain, were towed into port in Barbados. As no extradition treaty existed between Barbados and the UK, Biggs gratefully made his way back to Brazil. Eventually, it was ill-health, after suffering a series of heart attacks and strokes, that led to him voluntarily returning to face justice in England, after an absence of thirty-six years, in 2001. Held in Belmarsh high security prison in London, Biggs finally married Raimunda, so that his son could avoid expulsion as an illegal immigrant. Michael, who had enjoyed fleeting success as a child pop star in Brazil, conducted a campaign for his elderly ailing father's release and compassion was shown by the authorities when the prisoner was eventually freed two days before his 80th birthday in 2010. Unable to speak and using a word board to communicate with the press, Biggs launched an updated autobiography *Odd Man Out: The Last Straw* published in 2011. Shortly after being transferred from Belmarsh to Norwich Prison in 2009, Biggs echoed the words of criminal predecessor Edward Agar, when he released a statement condemning his life of crime:

I am an old man and often wonder if I truly deserve the extent of my punishment. I have accepted it and only want freedom to die with my family and not in jail. I hope Mr Shaw [then the Home Secretary] decides to allow me to do that. I have been in jail for a long time and I want to die a free man. I am sorry for what happened. It has not been an easy ride over the years. Even in Brazil I was a prisoner of my own making. There is no honour to being known as a Great Train Robber. My life has been wasted.

Criminal mastermind, Bruce Reynolds remained at large before an international manhunt came to an end in November 1968. The arrest was made by dogged Flying Squad Detective Chief Inspector Tommy Butler whose determination to bring his quarry to justice had delayed his retirement and extended his length of service by a year to complete the search. Charged with 'being concerned with others in the robbery of a Royal Mail Train', Reynolds served ten years of a twenty-five year sentence after being apprehended in a dawn raid mounted on his hideout in Torquay. The career criminal had spent the previous two months on the 'English Riviera', revisiting the seaside resort where he had spent childhood holidays with his father and step-mother. Accompanied by his wife Frances and their six year-old son Nicholas, who attended a private school in the town, the family resided at a rented luxury hilltop house with panoramic sea views. Reynolds still visited the London area to carry out crimes in a bid to fund a move to New Zealand, for, after five

---

Wanted

Bucks., Aylesbury Co.—ROBBERY. 3 a.m. 8th inst., at Cheddington, vide Case 42, 22-8-63. Stopped express train, attacked driver, entered travelling post office attached to train and stole 128 post bags containing about 2½ million pounds in currency (about £20,000 in Scottish and Irish notes). **BRUCE RICHARD REYNOLDS**, alias RAYMOND ETTRIDGE and GEORGE RACHEL, C.R.O. No. 41212-48, b. London 7-9-31, motor

Bruce Richard Reynolds (photograph taken 1960)

dealer/antique dealer, 6ft. 1in., c. fresh (slightly suntanned), h. lt. brown, e. grey (wears horn rimmed or rimless spectacles), fairly well spoken, slight cleft in chin, scar l. eyelid and cheek and rt. forearm. Cons. for larceny, assault on police, receiving, causing g.b.h. with intent, shop, house, workshopbreaking, etc. at Ongar and M.P. (C.O., C-8, C, F, L, P and W). Last, 30-5-63—fined. Is the holder of Passport No. C.206103, issued at Marseilles, France and during the past year has visited Gibraltar, Spain, Monte Carlo, Paris, North Africa.

Britain's most wanted man Bruce Reynolds.

years on the run, with periods spent in France, Canada and Mexico, his share of the train loot had dwindled from £150,000 to just £5,000. Living the good life, Reynolds and his wife had once quaffed a case of champagne every week but were now reduced to sipping sparingly from a single bottle of vodka.

Posing as an antiques dealer, Reynolds's transport was a stolen red and black mini with changed number plates, driven with an insurance cover note and a driving licence issued in a false name. Ten days before his capture, Reynolds had a slight brush with the law for parking too close to a zebra crossing. Although it was only a minor offence, a policeman asked him to produce his driving documents at Torquay police station. Calmly taking his son along with him, Britain's most wanted man was not recognised during the routine check. Using an alias, the robber had recently replaced his invalid international licence by taking a driving test at Newton Abbot. He passed despite his nervousness when the examiner revealed that he had previously spent thirty years as a member of the Flying Squad.

During his stay in Devon, a wave of nostalgia spurred the robber to proudly take his family on a strange pilgrimage to the scene of his greatest crime. He later recalled: 'Standing in the sunshine, staring at the strip of railway line, I explained exactly how the train was stopped, separated and then relieved of its contents. The magic of that night was still with me, even if the money had gone'.

'God save the Queen'

John Tawell escaped on the royal road
After administering a poison draft.
Fleeing from a crime on the royal road
He was hanged by the telegraph

A bullet missed the monarch on the royal road
Fired by Roderick Maclean.
For committing a crime on the royal road
He was found 'Not guilty, but insane'.

The attempt on Queen Victoria's life.

2

CRIME ON THE ROYAL ROAD

Royal Railway History

The Prince of Wales (who later abdicated as King Edward VIII) bequeathed upon the Great Western Railway the distinguished title of 'The Royal Road'. The first section of the line had opened a month before the Coronation of his great-grandmother, Queen Victoria, when the locomotive *North Star* travelled the twenty-five miles from Paddington to Maidenhead carrying a party of VIP's along the first completed section of Isambard Kingdom Brunel's Great Western Railway line on Thursday 31 May 1838. A correspondent of *The Sun* was impressed by the journey: 'This railway may well claim for itself the title "great", for it throws completely into the shade all those lines already open to the public'.

With the arrival of the railroad, famous personalities were able to use the new mode of transport to visit the sovereign at Windsor Castle, which was prominently visible from the Great Western Railway line. Amongst those early travellers was the Prime Minister, Sir Robert Peel; one of his predecessors the Duke of Wellington; and notably, Prince Albert of Saxe-Coburg-Gotha, who successfully wooed his cousin resulting in a royal marriage that took place in February1840. The Prince Consort readily embraced train travel, but many advisors considered it was too unsafe for the monarch. Her Majesty was finally coaxed into trying it by her husband on Monday 13 June 1842. The Great Western Railway company had already built a royal coach in anticipation of the royal patronage and the first train journey of a reigning British monarch was turned into a prestigious event. At noon the royal party left Slough for Paddington with Great Western Railway locomotive engineer Daniel Gooch at the controls

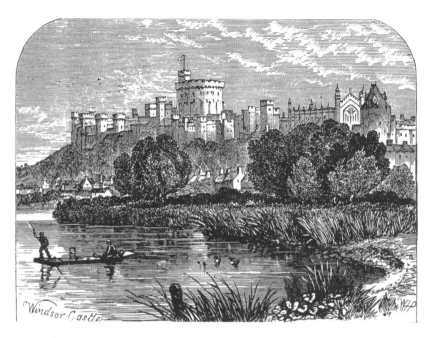

Home of the Monarch, Windsor Castle.

of the engine accompanied on the footplate by the line's creator Isambard Kingdom Brunel. The scene at Paddington Station was described in the *Windsor and Eton Express*: 'Precisely at 25 minutes past 12 o'clock the Royal Special train entered the terminus having performed the distance in 25 minutes, and on Her Majesty alighting she was given the most deafening demonstrations of loyalty and affection we ever experienced'.

When the Electric Magnetic Telegraph system devised by Wheatstone and Cooke was installed on the line between Slough and Paddington in 1844, it was utilised in August of that year to send a message to the Ministers of the Crown announcing the birth of Queen Victoria and Prince Albert's second son Prince Alfred (later titled the Duke of Edinburgh). At the beginning of the following year, the telegraph line was instrumental in bringing a Quaker, John Tawell, to justice for murder. The contribution of the new technology was acknowledged by the *Times*: 'It may be observed, that had it not been for the efficient aid of the electric telegraph, both at Slough and Paddington, the greatest difficulty as well as delay would have occurred in the apprehension of the party now in custody'.

The Slough Murder

The Great Western Railway telegraph system initiated a murder hunt by the following signal sent on New Year's Day 1845. There was no code for the letter 'Q', hence the letter 'K' was substituted and the word 'Quaker' modified to 'Kwaker':

Message from Slough:
A murder has just been committed at Salt Hill, and the suspected murderer was seen to take a first-class ticket for London by the train which left Slough at 7.42 p.m. He is in the garb of a Kwaker, with a brown great coat on, which reaches nearly down to his feet; he is in the last compartment of the second first-class carriage.
Reply from Paddington:
The up-train has arrived; and a person answering, in every respect, the description given by telegraph came out of the compartment mentioned. I pointed the man out to Sergeant Williams. The man got into a New Road omnibus, and Sergeant Williams into the same.

Duty Sergeant William Williams of the Great Western Railway police sat at the back of the bus and was surprised to be handed a fare by the suspect, who mistook him for the conductor, when he alighted near the Bank of England in Princes Street. Following at a discreet distance the sergeant observed the 'Kwaker' enter the Jerusalem Coffee House, which was a haunt for Australian

A telegraph message led to the capture of a murderer.

merchants, then make his way to a lodging house in Scott's Yard which provided accommodation exclusively for members of the Society of Friends. Satisfying himself that the man he was following was settled in for the night, Sergeant Williams returned to Paddington to receive further instructions after ascertaining exactly what had occurred at Salt Hill. It transpired that at about 6.30pm, a woman's screams had been heard coming from one of the four terraced houses in Bath Place. Taking a candle and rushing out of her house to investigate the noise, Mary Anne Ashley heard the front door of the house next door slam shut. Looking round she saw a man she recognised walking up the path. When he opened the gate she asked 'What is wrong with my neighbour; I am afraid she is ill'. The man made no reply and was visibly trembling as he hurried past her. Entering the house, Mrs Ashley, saw her friend Sarah Hart foaming at the mouth and writhing on the floor in agony. A doctor was called but nothing could be done for the victim of cyanide poisoning apparently administered in a glass of porter she had consumed.

The Reverend Champnes, hearing that a man dressed like a Quaker had been seen leaving the scene of a suspicious death, guessed correctly that the suspect must have gone to catch the train to London. He hurried to Slough and seeing a man dressed in a broad brimmed hat, white cravat and long coat, the vicar alerted the railway superintendent of his suspicions. When the Quaker boarded a first class carriage to London, a full description was telegraphed to Paddington and passed to Sergeant Williams.

The Metropolitan Police returned to the lodging house. The suspect had left his room but at lunchtime he was located and arrested at the Jerusalem Coffee House. The man taken into custody was John Tawell, aged sixty-one, who denied having visited Slough or knowing anyone there, but this was soon proved to be untrue. Sarah Hart, a forty-year-old mother of two children, a boy and a girl aged five and four respectively, had frequently been visited by Tawell. She told her friends and neighbours that she had worked as a servant for a Quaker couple and married their son against the wishes of his family. The husband was working abroad and arranged for the old gentleman Tawell to provide his family with money. This was also untrue, for Sarah Hart was unmarried and the father of her two children was none other than her elderly visitor and former employer John Tawell. The Quaker's life had been a litany of misdemeanours strangely at odds with his outwardly pious beliefs.

Born near Norwich in Norfolk, John Tawell had been introduced to the Society of Friends at the age of fourteen whilst working in a shop owned by a Quaker widow. Six years later he was working at a draper's shop in the Whitechapel area of London, owned by another Quaker, where he began a relationship with a serving girl called Mary who was soon expecting his child. The Quaker faith strongly disapproved of this lewd behaviour by two members of their community and the shamed lovers entered into belated wedlock. The couple had two sons before Tawell committed a sin against the Quaker community, which also violated the law of the land for which the penalty was death. Whilst working as a travelling salesman for a chemist, Tawell was committed for trial on charges connected with the forgery of banknotes. He had been arrested after trying to pass himself off as a partner of Smith's Bank of Uxbridge. Boldly visiting the bank's engraver he ordered a new plate to be made and 'specimens' of £5 notes bearing the name of Smith's Bank to be printed. When the customer was satisfied with the proofs he placed an order for a quantity of notes. By now the engraver's suspicions were aroused and when Tawell returned to pay the bill and collect the banknotes, the police were laying in wait and apprehended the fraudster as he left the shop. The owners of the bank were Quakers and this crime committed by one of their number left them in a quandary. The Society of Friends was opposed to the death penalty that Tawell now faced, as forgery was then a capital offence. The Smith family were relieved of the responsibility for such harsh justice and did not press charges when a forged banknote belonging to the Bank of England was found on Tawell's person. The accused was charged with 'feloniously falsely forging and counterfeiting a Bank-note for payment of 10 shillings [50p], with intent to defraud the Governor and Company of the Bank of England'.

When Tawell appeared at the Old Bailey on 4 February 1814, an admission to a lesser offence of 'possession' was accepted and the prisoner was considered extremely fortunate to avoid execution for forgery and fraud. As a consequence a comparatively 'lenient' sentence of fourteen years transportation was imposed. For the first few years of his sentence, the prisoner was assigned to labouring on coal ships working around the coast of Australia. His knowledge

Prisoner John Tawell.

of medicines, learned while working for the chemist in London, won him a position in a convict hospital, followed by a spell at the Sydney Academy as a clerk. The principal, Isaac Wood, was impressed by the convict's faith and intelligence and petitioned for

Tawell's parole, which was granted half way through the sentence in 1820. With his unexpected freedom, Tawell then displayed astonishing entrepreneurial flair by establishing a successful business as a chemist and druggist in Sydney. From this base he quickly amassed a personal fortune of over £20,000 from land, property and the shipping trade. Although, aligning himself closely with the local Quaker community in Sydney, his conscience was apparently not troubled by taking a mistress in the colony until his wife and children sailed out to join him in 1823. The couple added a daughter to their family and decided to return to England in November 1831. John Tawell had earned wealth and respectability and was given a warm send-off by his business associates which was reported by the *Sydney Gazette*:

On the evening of Saturday last, about 20 respectable colonists gave a farewell dinner, at Hart's tavern, to Mr Tawell, an old and esteemed resident in Sydney, who is about to return to England by the first vessel. Mr Samuel Terry presided on the occasion, and was well supported by Mr Simpson Lord as vice-president. After the cloth was removed, and the usual loyal toasts were drunk, the president after some appropriate remarks, proposed the health of Mr Tawell, who returned thanks for the honour conferred upon him by so many respectable gentlemen, assuring the company that whether he should return to the colony, or remain in England, the recollection of their kindness would ever be to him one of the greatest pleasures of his life. The health of Mrs Tawell and family was also drunk, and acknowledgements in suitable terms by Mr Tawell. Several songs were sung in the course of the evening, and the company broke up about 11 o'clock, after enjoying one of the most convivial parties ever witnessed in the colony. The object of the entertainment, that of paying a well-deserved tribute of respect to an old colonist, now about to bid perhaps a final adieu to our shores, was not more creditable to the guest than to those by whom so high a compliment was paid to him. We ought to add, that Mr Hart, by providing a very excellent dinner, contributed his share to the enjoyment of the evening.

There were tragic consequences of the family's return to England. The appalling social conditions in Victorian London affected the health of the Tawell's youngest son William who died in 1833. The following year the bereaved parents returned to Australia and in 1837 the first Friends Meeting House opened in Sydney with a plaque bearing the donor's name 'John Tawell - to the Society of Friends'. The Tawells final journey home in July 1838 coincided with the death of their married son John, who had remained in England to train as a doctor. This blow was too much to bear for the grief stricken Mary Tawell who became gravely ill and her husband employed a young nurse Sarah Lawrence to care for his wife at their home in Berkhampstead, Hertfordshire. As Mary's life ebbed away, Tawell turned for comfort to Sarah and soon after his wife's death the servant girl was expecting his child and moved away to give birth to a son called Frederick. The name of the father was kept secret but Tawell continued seeing Sarah and when she became pregnant again, it was an inconvenience to the religious hypocrite, who by this time planned to marry a highly respectable widow, Sarah Cutworth, a Quaker who ran a school for young ladies. After giving birth to a daughter she named after herself, Sarah Lawrence changed her surname to Hart and agreed to shield her master from embarrassment by moving to Slough. For her trouble she received an allowance from the children's father of £1 a week.

Tawell's criminal past meant that he had never been fully accepted back into the fold by the London Society of Friends despite his numerous acts of generosity to worthy causes. Ignoring the warnings of her friends and family in the Quaker community, the widow Cutworth gave up her school and married Tawell at a registry office in February 1841. The marriage was not sanctioned by the Quaker movement, therefore both partners of the union were designated 'outward court worshippers'. Living with the newly-weds was a daughter from each of their previous marriages and soon the family had an addition when the couple produced a son. Increasingly, Tawell was worried that his illicit relationship with a former servant might come to light. He was overdrawn at the bank while experiencing difficulties with his business interests in

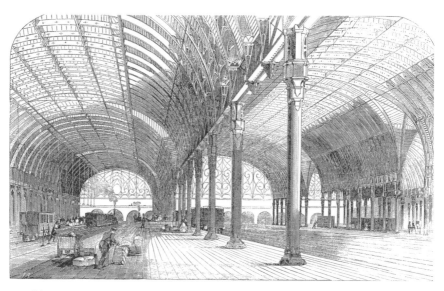

Paddington Station.

Australia and decided to use his knowledge of poisons to eliminate one of his financial burdens - Sarah Hart.

The first attempt to kill his former lover ended in failure. During a visit to deliver maintenance in September 1844, Sarah vomited after drinking a glass of stout, which she believed she had drunk too quickly, not knowing that it contained a drug administered by her malevolent benefactor. Next time, the murderer made sure his evil intention was successfully carried out. On New Year's Day 1845, Tawell entered a chemist's shop in Bishopsgate Street and purchased a preparation normally prescribed to treat varicose veins that contained deadly prussic acid (cyanide). Travelling across London to Paddington, he caught the 4pm train to Slough and went to see his secret family at their home in Salt Hill. Sarah was pleased to see him, as her quarterly allowance was overdue. She went out to the nearby Windmill Hotel, purchased a bottle of Guinness and borrowed a corkscrew opener, which she promised, 'You may depend on my returning in the morning'. The stout was poured into two glasses and Tawell managed to distract Sarah long enough to lace the drink with a lethal dose of poison that took immediate effect. The killer paused to take back his maintenance money then fled from the scene. After boarding the 7.42 to Paddington his carefully planned escape was foiled by the smart use of the telegraph system. Unaware of the fact that he had been shadowed, Tawell protested his innocence when arrested at the Jerusalem Coffee House assuring the officers 'I wasn't at Slough yesterday'. Sergeant Williams replied, 'Yes you were sir, you got out of the train and got into an omnibus and gave me the change'. Seemingly un-phased by this revelation, Tawell confidently retorted, 'You must be mistaken in the identity; my station in society will be sufficient to rebut any suspicion against me'.

Once in the custody of the Eton police, Tawell admitted knowing the victim and suggested that she had committed suicide in a statement to Superintendent Perkins:

That wretched and unfortunate woman once lived in my service for nearly two years and a half. I was pestered with letters from her when I was in London and I determined to give her no more money. She was a bad woman - a very bad woman. She sent me a letter threatening to do something. She said she would make away with herself if I did not give her any money. I went down to her house and told her I would not give her any more money. She then asked me to give her a drop of porter. She had a glass, and I had a glass. She held in her hand over the glass of porter a very small phial, not bigger than her finger and said, 'I will, I will!' She poured something out of the phial into the stout and drank part of it. She then lay down on the rug and I walked out. I should not have gone out if I thought she had been in earnest. I certainly should not have left her.

The trial opened at the Buckinghamshire Assizes held at Aylesbury County Court on 12 March 1845 presided over by Judge Baron Parke. The prosecution produced a witness who knew the full story of the secretive affair between master and servant. Charlotte Howard, a carpenter's wife from Paddington, was a friend of

Sarah's and had visited the couple's first love nest in Bridge Street, Southwark:

I knew Sarah Hart. About six years ago she went to nurse the first Mrs Tawell. Mrs Tawell died about nine or ten weeks after she went to nurse her, and deceased remained in the service of the prisoner. About five years ago she told me she was in the family way. I remember on one occasion taking tea there with the prisoner. Sarah brought in the tea and took the things away again. She then came in and sat down by my side. I said 'I know Sarah what you are going to speak about'. She got up and showed a disposition to vindicate her master. In June 1840, he said he was about to get married to Mrs Cutworth and if these things were rumoured about it would make a very great difference. He laughed and begged Sarah not to excite herself so much; he said he was about to be admitted as a Friend, and should not like her latest pregnancy to be talked about. She said she would be dead to the world from that time; that no-one would know what became of her, not even her own mother.

The jury heard how two visits from Tawell had affected Sarah Hart's health. The victim had supplemented her income by caring for the illegitimate child of servant Charlotte Howard who was staying with Sarah on the first occasion that she had been taken poorly:

On 26 September 1843 I went to stay with Mrs Hart at Bath Place. I was then in the family way and gave birth there. I remained there four months. During that time I saw Mr Tawell two or three times. I went to the house last September again. My child was there. I got leave of absence from my mistress to go and see my child for a fortnight. I remember Mr Tawell coming down on the 30 September 1844, shortly before 7pm in the evening. I did not see him but heard his voice. He stayed there about 40 minutes. I was told by Mrs Hart to go and get a bottle of porter, which I did. I then saw Mrs Hart again; she came out of the room and said 'I am very ill, I was obliged to tell my master to go, for I can scarce stand'. She looked dreadfully pale and ill, retched a good deal, and complained about being sick in the head. Before that she was in sound health. She went upstairs and partly recovered by taking rest; but in the night she again complained of being sick, and retched much. She retched altogether about a full hand basin. She said she had drunk a glass of porter, and she was sorry she had drunk it all at once, for it had affected her head immediately, and made her feel very giddy. On coming downstairs I observed on the table in the room where Mr Tawell had been: 13 sovereigns, half a bottle of porter and two glasses. I drank some of the remaining porter but it did not make me feel sick.

First on the scene of the murder was widow Mary Anne Ashley who heard the victim's screams and saw Tawell leave before she entered the house to witness Sarah Hart's death throes:

I found her lying upon her back on the floor, with her clothes nearly up to her knees, and the stocking on her left leg nearly down and torn. Her cap was off her head, and she appeared to have been struggling. She was alive and making a moaning cry. I bathed her temples with vinegar and water. On the table in the room were a bottle and a tumbler, both containing some beer, and also a jug of water. When I lifted her up she was foaming at the mouth. Another neighbour, Mrs Barrett, came in and used the empty glass to give water to the deceased. I said, 'She cannot swallow; don't give her any, it will choke her'.

Tawell objected to paying £1 a week to support his illegitimate family but spared no expense on his legal costs that were estimated to be in excess of £700. He engaged eminent advocate Sir Fitzroy Kelly who had tears in his eyes as he made an emotional plea to the jury on behalf of an 'innocent man'. After first suggesting that the deceased may have been poorly and choked to death when the neighbour poured water down her throat, he also came up with an alternative suspect in his address to the jury - apple pips! A post mortem examination had revealed pieces of undigested apple in the victim's stomach. As minute traces of cyanide are present in apple pips, the devious lawyer attempted to convince the court that a diet of too much fruit over the festive season had brought about the premature death of Sarah Hart: 'What were the jury called upon to believe? A woman in health had died suddenly, and the prosecutor asked the jury to take away the life of the prisoner on the supposition that she had died from prussic acid and not any one of the many causes of sudden death. What was the quantity of prussic acid required to cause death? It might be un-dissolved apples, bitter almonds or anything else containing prussic acid. I wish to impress upon the jury, that, next to bitter almonds, there is no substance which contains more prussic acid than the pips of apples, the quantity differing according to the nature of the apple'.

This revelation was said to have had a detrimental affect on the sale of apples, but the jury were unimpressed by this explanation of a cause of death. The jurors already had the 'pip' and complained to the Judge about the standard of their accommodation where there were no beds and they had been forced to sleep on the floor. After putting up with this nightly discomfort and hearing evidence for three days they retired to consider their verdict and required only half-an-hour for their deliberations before they returned a verdict of 'Guilty'.

Unlike members of the jury, the condemned man was provided with a bed; in fact he was chained to it throughout his confinement, but nevertheless, observed the proprieties by writing a letter of thanks to the Governor of Aylesbury Prison, Mr Sheriff:

Dear and worthy friend, Mr. Sheriff, It is not less my duty to than great pleasure, as well as from feelings of deep and sincere gratitude, that I can thus offer my poor but unqualified thanks to both thyself and poor Mrs. Sheriff for the continued and marked kind attention which has been shown so uniformly to myself and my dear and valuable family and friends since my unfortunate confinement in this prison, by allowing us all the access which urbanity and philanthropy could suggest, under such circumstances, to the participants in this severe affliction.

And now their deeply distressing probation is nearly concluded, I have to desire that this may be accepted as the most grateful acknowledgement, both on account of myself and them.

I can desire myself that the Divine blessing may largely rest on thyself, and Mrs. Sheriff, and your family; and my own valuable family will lastingly have to re-echo this poor but sincere benediction of thy faithful but afflicted friend.

John Tawell.

The Governor and the Prison Chaplain, the Reverend Cox, sat up praying with Tawell on the night before his execution. Having convinced his wife, brother and concerned members of the Society of Friends that he was totally innocent of the charge, the sanctimonious killer kept up the pretence to visitors right up to the day of the execution. At 5am the governor reminded the condemned man that his time was drawing near and broached the subject of a confession, 'Mr Tawell, I think there was some promise made me of a statement you intended leaving'. The prisoner replied, 'If I promised then I will do so' and produced a piece of paper, which he gave to the chaplain with the proviso that the contents should not be made public. He then sat down in the cell and admitted: 'Yes, I am guilty of the crime. I put the prussic acid into the porter, and I also attempted the crime in September last, not by prussic acid, but morphia'.

Hangman William Calcraft was appointed to conduct the public execution at 8am on Friday 28 March. A temporary scaffold was erected by fixing a platform on top of the iron railings of the balcony at the county hall that stood alongside the prison. Pressmen noted that there was a disappointing turnout of only 'two or three thousand persons present' mainly 'agricultural workers' and women of 'questionable character'. The crowd were kept waiting for over

The hangman, William Calcraft.

65

twenty minutes after the appointed hour before the bewildered figure of the condemned man was pushed out into view by a turnkey. The prisoner, still attired in the dress of a Quaker, clasped his handcuffed hands together and dropped to one knee continually repeating a brief prayer, 'Sweet Jesus, receive my spirit', before being hauled to his feet by the impatient Calcraft. The undignified proceedings were described by a correspondent of the *Times*:

When the fixing of the rope had been properly completed... the executioner and the turnkey withdrew into the hall, and the bolts sustaining the platform on which the wretched man stood were instantly pulled back, and he fell; but the length of the drop allowed him was so little, that he struggled most violently. His whole frame was convulsed; he writhed horribly, and his limbs rose and fell again repeatedly, while he continued to wring his hands for several minutes, they still being clasped as though he had not left off praying. It was nearly ten minutes after the rope had been fixed before the contortions, which indicated his extreme suffering ceased. ... He died 'hard', as the phrase is; and his light body dangled in the breeze, backwards and forwards, and round about, a most pitiable and melancholy spectacle. ... And the removal of the body was quite consistent with the rest of the revolting exhibition, for it was not cut down, but the turnkey held up the legs while the executioner, untied the rope, which was certainly a new cut, and probably considered worth saving for some purpose or other.

The sensational nature of the case provided excellent publicity for the Wheatstone and Cooke invention and the telegraph offices at Slough and Paddington became an extremely popular visitor attraction as the public, 'who dearly love anything connected with a murder, flocked to see the new apparatus at work, cheerfully paying their shillings [5p] for the privilege of doing so'. A former Lieutenant-Governor of Canada, Sir Francis Head, also recalled that the historic crime stimulated rare comment in a railway carriage: 'A few months afterwards, we happened to be travelling by rail from Paddington to Slough in a carriage filled with people all strangers

The Wheatstone and Cooke telegraph office became a visitor attraction.

to one another. Like English travellers they were all mute. For nearly fifteen miles no one had uttered a single word, until a short-bodied, short-necked, short-nosed, exceedingly respectable-looking man in the corner, fixing his eyes on the apparently fleeting posts and wires of the electric telegraph, significantly nodded to us as he muttered aloud - "Them's the cords that hung John Tawell"'.

Queen Victoria's Station Assassin

In 1882, Queen Victoria was the target of an outrageous crime and sent a telegram to her eldest son playing down the details of an attempt on her life at Windsor railway station:

From the Queen, Windsor Castle, to the Prince of Wales, Marlborough House.
In case exaggerated report should reach you, I telegraph to say that as I drove from the station here a man shot at the carriage, but fortunately hit no one. He was instantly arrested. I am none the worse.

The official Court Circular issued from Windsor Castle also described the incident that shocked the world in a matter-of-fact manner:

The Queen, accompanied by Princess Beatrice and attended by the Dowager Duchess of Roxburghe and the Equerries in Waiting, arrived at the Castle at half past five p.m. yesterday from London.
As the Queen left the station at Windsor, in a closed carriage, a man who was standing in the crowd, fired a shot from a revolver at her Majesty, and was instantly secured.
The Queen heard the report, but did not see the occurrence, but Princess Beatrice, who was sitting on that side of the carriage, perceived the man raise his hand and fire.
The Queen, who was not alarmed, drove on to the Castle, and sent to make enquiries whether any one had been hurt.
Her Majesty is very well today and has not suffered from the shock.

On Thursday 2 March, the royal train had travelled from

Roderick Maclean shoots at the royal carriage.

Paddington and arrived at Windsor at 5.25pm. Queen Victoria and her daughter Princess Beatrice walked from the station and boarded a waiting horse-driven carriage. As the vehicle pulled away, the cheers of the assembled crowd turned to shrieks of horror when a gunman stepped forward and fired a revolver. The bullet passed

Maclean is driven away in a cab following his arrest.

narrowly past the head of the sovereign's favourite servant, John Brown, who was standing guard on the rear of the carriage.

Before a second shot could be fired, the would-be assassin was overpowered by George Hayes, superintendent of police at Windsor (later awarded the sum of £5 by the sovereign in recognition of his bravery). The police officer was assisted by two quick-thinking pupils from Eton College, one of whom landed several fierce blows on the gunmen with a folded umbrella. The pistol was then wrested from the gunman's hand by photographer, James Burnside. The prisoner pleaded with Superintendent Hayes, 'Don't hurt me, I'll go quietly', before being bundled in to a cab just in time to escape the attentions of an angry mob seeking instant retribution for the crime.

As the royal carriage sped away to the safety of Windsor Castle, a furious crowd surrounded and followed the vehicle shielding the villain to the nearby police station. The culprit was identified as twenty-seven-year-old, Roderick Maclean, a London man from a good family whose eccentric behaviour since the death of his parents had led him to lead what was described as 'an idle and aimless life'.

Although reasonably well-educated, he had no actual trade or profession and following temporary spells of employment as a shop worker or a clerk, had wandered the country eking out an existence on handouts obtained from his family. Shabbily dressed in threadbare trousers, well-worn overcoat and dilapidated round hat, the prisoner claimed that poverty had driven him to desperate measures and he had shot at the royal carriage in order to draw attention to his plight, pleading 'I have done it through starvation'.

On his person was found only a penny and three farthings (now worth less than 1p), however, it was discovered that he had recently bought the revolver from Portsmouth for five shillings and sixpence (17p). Maclean's previous landlady, Mrs Hucker of Southsea, bluntly told the press that she had always regarded her lodger as having 'a tile loose'. Before leaving her home, the prisoner had sold her a concertina and a woollen comforter so that, in his own words (which later proved to have a far more sinister meaning), 'I might have something in my pocket'.

When the weapon purchased by Maclean was examined by the police, the six chambered medium-sized revolver still remained loaded with two ball cartridges. A further fourteen cartridges were found in the prisoner's pockets. It was also discovered that, while waiting for the royal train to arrive, Maclean had sat in the waiting room at Windsor station and scribbled a note in pencil outlining a perceived grievance against his sister who lived in Croydon. She had recently upset him by reducing the amount of money she regularly forwarded to him in postal orders as a living allowance. Signed and dated, the letter was retrieved from the prisoner's pocket during a search conducted by the police following the assassin's arrest:

The prisoner being questioned at Windsor police station.

I should not have done this crime had you, as you should have done, allowed the 10 shillings [50p] per week instead of offering the insultingly small sum of 6 shillings [30p] a week and expecting me to live on it. So you perceive the great good a little money might have done, had you not treated me as a fool and set me more than ever against those bloated aristocrats ruled by the old lady, Mrs Vic [the queen], who is a licensed robber in all senses.

A solicitor acting on behalf of Maclean's family revealed details of the prisoner's troubled background in a letter to the editor of the *Times*:

I am professionally concerned for the family of the unfortunate man whom I have seen this afternoon. He is manifestly insane, and has recently been discharged from a lunatic asylum in Wells, in Somersetshire, and for many years he has not been responsible for his actions, one of which was an attempt to wreck a railway train.

This earlier incident referred to by the solicitor occurred on the London, Chatham and Dover Railway at Ewell in August 1874. Roderick Maclean, then aged eighteen, incited a twelve year-old boy, John Cheeseman to place a piece of chalk on the line by offering him a halfpenny. When a train passed over the chalk and crushed it, Maclean then tried to entice the younger boy to place a wooden sleeper on the line for the sum of sixpence. The sleeper, however, proved too heavy for Cheeseman to lift and he was unable to move it. Despite the fact that there was no harm done, as a result of their mischief, the youths were arrested and brought to trial at the Assizes held in Maidstone that year in December. John Cheeseman was charged with two counts of 'intent thereby to endanger the safety of persons travelling upon the railway', while Roderick Maclean faced charges of inciting him to commit the offences.

Upon hearing the evidence, the judge ordered an acquittal but warned the two boys about their future conduct. The judge made it clear that in his mind Maclean had misled the other prisoner. Furthermore, if Cheeseman had succeeded in

Roderick Maclean claimed he did not shoot to kill.

placing the sleeper on the line and passengers had been killed, then both culprits would have been tried for wilful murder. If that grim outcome had been the case, Maclean may well have faced the prospect of the death penalty.

Since that early brush with the law, Roderick Maclean had spent periods in asylums in Dublin, Wells and Weston-super-Mare. Only a month before committing the crime that brought him notoriety, his application to a medical officer for admission to an infirmary in the London area was refused and when directed to the relieving officer of the workhouse, the sick young man declined the order and began to curse the Queen, vowing she should suffer for his ill-treatment. Roderick Maclean had harboured ambitions to become a poet and had earlier submitted loyal verses to Queen Victoria that had been rebuffed when an official returned them stating that Her Majesty always declined to accept such offering from her subjects - an action that further fuelled his simmering resentment against the sovereign.

While awaiting trial for the attempted assassination to commence, Maclean worked feverishly on an autobiography entitled 'The History of My Life' and, in the vain hope that one day he would regain his liberty, described his actions in this latest sorry episode:

> *I merely fired at her Majesty's carriage, not her Majesty. The Princess Beatrice was also in the carriage; so according to the circumstances and suppositions I may have had designs against her; so, I cannot see why the people should charge me with the intention of shooting her Majesty with intent to murder more especially as any murderous intentions towards any one were not in my mind.*

Nevertheless, despite his protestations of innocence, the prisoner was charged with being 'a false traitor, guilty of high treason in that he on the 2 March, in this year, did shoot off and discharge a pistol loaded with gunpowder and bullets against the person of our lady the Queen, with intent to maliciously kill and put to death out lady the Queen'. The day after his arrest, Maclean had made a full statement to the police outlining his defence:

The prisoner was found 'not guilty, but insane'.

I am not guilty of the charge of shooting with the intention of causing actual bodily harm. My object was, by frightening her Majesty the Queen, to alarm the public, with the result of having my grievances respected, viz,, such as the pecuniary straits in which I have been situated. All the circumstances tend to prove this statement. Firstly, had I intended to injure the Queen I should have fired at her when she was quitting the railway carriage. Quite on the contrary, I pointed the pistol on a level with the wheels, but as I felt a slight kick, doubtless the contents may have lodged in one of the doors. If her Majesty will accept this explanation, and allow the words with the intent of 'intimidating others', instead of 'causing bodily harm', to be inserted in the indictment, in that event I will offer all the assistance in my power to bring the charge I herein specify to a speedy issue. I hope her Majesty will accept the only consolation I can offer - namely, I had no intention whatever of causing any injury.

At the Crown Court of the Reading Assizes, the prosecution called for the death penalty, but, after hearing testimony from several medical experts called by the defence, the jury took just five minutes to return a verdict of 'not guilty, on the ground of insanity'. As a result, the judge ordered the accused to be detained during Her Majesty's pleasure. The satirical magazine *Punch* summed up the case succinctly with a comic verse:

> *Roderick Maclean*
> *He shot at the Queen*
> *The jury took 'reason'*
> *Out of his treason*
> *So Rod'rick Maclean*
> *Was pronounced insane*

However, Queen Victoria was not so amused about the contradictory verdict of 'not guilty but insane' and initiated a change in the law that changed the form of such verdicts in future cases to be judged 'guilty but insane'.

This was the seventh and final time that the sovereign was confronted by youthful gunmen during her reign. The first occasion occurred in June 1840, when a coffee shop waiter named Edward Oxford fired a pistol at the Queen and the Prince Consort as the recently-wed royal couple were being driven in a carriage on Constitution Hill in Green Park. Tried for high treason, the culprit was declared insane, sent to an asylum for life, before being transferred to Broadmoor Prison for the criminally insane where he died.

Two further attempts took place at virtually the same spot in June 1842, when John Francis succeeded in escaping after his gun failed to fire, before he tried again by returning the following day. On this

John Francis shoots at Queen Victoria and Prince Albert, 1842.

occasion he walked boldly towards the royal carriage and discharged a pistol in the direction of Her Majesty. He was immediately seized and, with no plea of insanity, tried for high treason and sentenced to death - later commuted to life imprisonment on Norfolk Island. A month later, crippled William Bean, pointed a pistol at the royal carriage carrying the Queen, Prince Albert and the King of the Belgians. However, the barrel of the weapon contained only paper and a few grains of gunpowder which did not even cause a flash when fired. For this criminal folly, the young man was sentenced to eighteen months imprisonment.

A similar incident occurred in 1849, when an unemployed Irishman, William Hamilton was transported overseas for seven years after firing a blank shot at the Queen. In 1872, 'weak-minded' Arthur O'Connor accosted the royal carriage as it was entering Buckingham Palace. Waving a gun in one hand and a petition to release Fenian prisoners in the other, he terrified the Queen who later revealed how seriously the incident had affected her: 'I was trembling very much and a sort of shiver ran through me'. The

Gunman William Hamilton is apprehended in 1843.

assailant's weapon proved harmless, containing nothing more lethal than a greasy rag, but the monarch's manservant, John Brown, did not know that when he bravely seized the offender. For this act of bravery, John Brown was rewarded with public thanks, a gold medal and an annuity of £25. For his act of stupidity, the crazed youth Arthur O'Connor received twenty strokes of the birch rod and twelve months imprisonment.

Following the shooting incident involving Roderick Maclean, The *Penny Illustrated* reported the relief felt around the world for Queen Victoria's safe deliverance: 'It is needless to say that this attempt to destroy the life of the Sovereign, which, like others, has providentially failed at the supreme moment of the well-planned execution, has excited the most profound feelings of detestation and abhorrence of the act in the minds of the loyal and peaceful residents of the Royal borough, as indeed it has throughout the British Empire'. The Queen received the boys of Eton in the quadrangle of Windsor Castle and was presented with an address expressing 'feelings of loyalty and devotion' signed by the whole school. Her Majesty then personally thanked George Chesney Wilson and Leslie Melville Roberts, the two boys who had conspicuously distinguished themselves by grappling with the railway assassin.

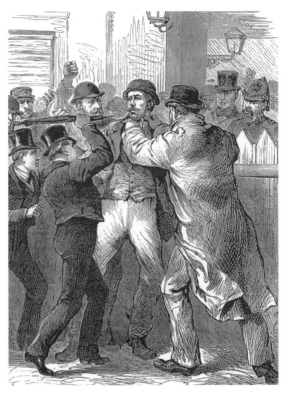

Maclean was attacked by an Eton schoolboy wielding an umbrella.

Another, perhaps less welcome, example of the outpouring of sympathy and affection for the Queen came from 'poet' William McGonagall, lauded as 'the writer of the worst poetry in the English language'.

He paid a tribute thanking God for sparing the monarch's life. An extract of the excruciating verses read:

> *God prosper long our noble Queen,*
> *And long may she reign!*
> *Maclean he tried to shoot her,*
> *But it was all in vain.*

For God He turned the ball aside
Maclean aimed at her head;
And he felt very angry
Because he didn't shoot her dead.

Maclean must be a madman,
Which is obvious to be seen,
Or else he wouldn't have tried to shoot
Our most beloved Queen.

Victoria is a good Queen,
Which all her subjects know,
And for that God has protected her
From all her deadly foes.

The Queen's birthday, celebrated on 5 June that year with the traditional Trooping the Colour on Horse Guards Parade, was a cause for special celebration as reported in the *Morning Post*:

The birthday of the Queen has not probably since her accession to the Throne been celebrated more generally or with more manifestations of loyalty and affection than it was on Saturday throughout the length and breadth of the country, and it was evident that the feeling of thankfulness that the Queen had been preserved from the danger that threatened her life at Windsor entered largely into the commemoration.

Victoria, recognising the worldwide indignation and public outpouring of loyalty at home, instigated by the assassination attempt, viewed the terrifying experience philosophically and subsequently wrote to her eldest daughter, Victoria, the Crown Princess of Prussia, 'It is worth being shot at - to see how much one is loved'.

3

FIRST CLASS RAILWAY MURDERS

Francis Muller doffed his hat
Then snatched a walking stick
He hit out time and time again
And killed poor Mr Briggs

Percy Lefroy doffed his hat
To impress the judge and jury
He confessed time and time again
But was shown no mercy

Jack the Ripper doffed his hat
Then slashed his victim's throat
He did it time and time again
And the villain was never caught

'Gentlemen, this is no way for first class passengers to behave'

Top Hat and Rails

Jack the Ripper depicted smartly dressed complete with top hat.

Fashions have changed dramatically among the criminal fraternity since the Nineteenth Century The stereotypical image of the modern-day knife-wielding or gun-toting assailant is of a youthful male 'hoodie' clad in tracksuit and designer trainers, listening to music downloads through his earphones as he threatens his victim. During the Victorian Age no self-respecting villain would have been seen, either on the street or in a railway carriage, unless appropriately attired in a suit, neck-tie and hat. In the case of three celebrated murderers, Franz Muller, Percy Lefroy and Jack the Ripper, the killers were distinguished by their apparent preference for a silk top hat!

The First Railway Carriage Murder

A mix-up over a pair of hats provided vital clues in apprehending the killer of the first railway carriage victim of murder, Thomas Briggs. The elderly chief clerk, of a bank in the City of London, was travelling to his home in Hackney by train on Saturday 9 July 1864. After finishing work that day, he had dined with his niece and her husband at their home in Peckham before taking an omnibus from the Old Kent Road to Fenchurch Street railway station. He then boarded the first class carriage of a North London Railway train, departing five minutes late at 9.50pm. It was only a short journey to his destination at Hackney Wick, but

Thomas Briggs.

when the train arrived, the seventy-year-old passenger had mysteriously disappeared.

By a strange coincidence, Semple Jones and Harry Verney, employees of the very same city bank as Thomas Briggs, entered the deserted first class compartment and, upon discovering it was covered in pools of blood, alerted a guard. Meanwhile, a driver travelling in the opposite direction between Hackney Wick and Bow, spotted a 'dark mound' near the railway line and upon drawing up to investigate further, discovered the missing banker lying injured on an embankment alongside the tracks. Thomas Briggs was barely alive, bleeding heavily from wounds inflicted to his head by a blunt instrument. He was carried to the Mitford Castle public house in Hackney and survived a further agonising twenty-four hours before losing his fight for life. The victim had been viciously beaten and robbed, then thrown out through a window of the moving train. Death was due to skull fractures and injuries to the brain. Suicide was quickly ruled out, as the most serious wounds were not consistent with a fall from a carriage.

It soon became apparent that a senseless murder had been committed in order to steal a gold watch with an Albert chain and a pair of gold spectacles. The thief had hastily disposed of the body, without relieving his hapless victim of other valuables, as reported by the first policeman on the scene, PC Edward Dougar:

I searched his pockets to ascertain who he was. His shirt front was rumpled and there was one black stud in it. A bunch of keys, four sovereigns, and some silver were in his left hand breeches pocket and in the other another bunch of keys and 8s 6d [42p] in silver and coppers. In his waist coat pocket there was a first class return ticket, and in his coat pocket I found his letters, papers and a silver snuff box. There was a patent fastening attached to his waist pocket for a gold chain, and there was a diamond ring upon his finger. There was no watch or chain on him.

The murder hunt, bolstered by a total reward of £300 offered by the police, railway company and Mr Brigg's employer, began with a search of the train carriage where the attack had occurred. Found in the bloodstained compartment was a walking stick (used as the murder weapon) and a bag belonging to the victim. Curiously, the banker's silk top hat was missing, however, in its place was a beaver hat apparently left behind by the fleeing killer. A description of the unidentified hat was circulated by the press and, nine days after the crime had been committed, an important witness, cab driver, Jonathan Matthews, came forward and stated that, in late 1863, he had bought one similar to his own, for his sister's then boyfriend, a thirty-year-old German tailor, Francis 'Franz' Muller:

I believe this to be the hat that I purchased for him; it corresponds exactly - before I bought it, out of the shop I had it turned up a little at each side - after I had purchased it I said I should like it turned up the same as the one I had the week previous, consequently they did it while I was there - I noticed that there was a little curl in the brim.

Another important development occurred on 20 July, when German immigrant, John Haffa, a fellow lodger and former work colleague of Franz Muller, produced a pawn ticket for a gold watch chain, purchased from the latter for 12 shillings (60p). The pledge, worth 30 shillings (£1.50), had been sold at a loss by Muller. The tailor had been dismissed from his job after an argument with the foreman and needed money for a passage to New York. Upon arriving in America, he told friends that he intended to enlist in the Union Army to fight against the South in the Civil War. The police followed up

Franz Muller.

this line of inquiry and discovered that the watch chain stolen from Mr Briggs, had been exchanged for another at a jeweller's shop in Cheapside, owned by John Death who recalled:

On Monday morning, July 11, a young man of about 30, with a foreign accent and having neither beard, moustache nor whiskers, of a pale sallow complexion and rather fair I should think, entered the shop around 10 o'clock. He took a chain from his pocket, apparently not attached to his watch, and asked him if I would let him have a new Albert chain for it of about the same value. Although having a foreign accent, he spoke English so plainly that I perfectly understood him. He wanted to have a new chain, without having to pay any money, for the old one, which was of the best description of gold.

Having disposed of the stolen chain, Muller had pawned the one received in exchange, then sold the pawn ticket to John Haffa. Within hours of this important breakthrough, having discovered

The police found incriminating evidence in Muller's luggage.

that Franz Muller had sailed for America on 15 July, two police officers, Detective Inspector Tanner and Detective Sergeant Clarke, set off in pursuit accompanied by key witnesses John Death and John Matthews. With a warrant for the arrest of Franz Muller, the four men boarded the steamship, *The City of Manchester*, and completed their voyage in time to meet the slower moving vessel, SS *Victoria*, carrying the fugitive.

Upon Muller's arrival on 24 August, the murder victim's watch and hat were found amongst his belongings and, following extradition proceedings, the prisoner was escorted back to England on board the steamship *Etna* and arrived to face justice on 17 September.

The trial commenced on 27 October and, despite a spirited defence of Muller, paid for by the accused man's countrymen, the German Legal Protection Society, the circumstantial evidence was overwhelming. On the third day, the jury retired, then returned within fifteen minutes to record a verdict of 'Guilty'. According to

The trial of Franz Muller.

the *Daily News*, trial judge, Baron Martin, 'placing on his head the hideously grotesquely black cap which tells that the wearer is about to pass the doom of violent and untimely death on a hapless fellow creature' pronounced the penalty of death, that was subsequently carried out despite a direct appeal for clemency from the King of Prussia to Queen Victoria. The case against the defendant was succinctly summed up in this extract from a broadside ballad entitled *The Lamentation of Franz Muller*:

> *That fatal night I was determined,*
> *Poor Thomas Briggs to rob and slay*
> *And in the fatal railway carriage,*
> *That night I took his life away.*

Baron Martin passing sentence of death on Franz Muller.

> *His crimson gore did stain the carriage,*
> *I threw him from the same, alack!*
> *I on the railway left him bleeding,*
> *I robbed him of his watch and hat.*
>
> *I never thought the law would take me,*
> *When I sailed o'er the raging main*
> *All my courage did forsake me,*
> *A murderer in the railway train.*

Franz Muller claimed he had bought the watch and chain from someone whose name he didn't know and that the hat he was wearing when arrested was not the one taken from the railway carriage. Further doubt about Franz Muller's guilt, was engendered by the fact that no witness had seen him in the vicinity of the North London Railway on the evening of the murder. In his defence, Muller claimed that he had travelled by omnibus to Camberwell on the fateful night to see his 'sweetheart' who had subsequently turned down the opportunity to travel to America with him. However, this witness was Mary Ann Eldred, a prostitute, who simply thought of Muller as another client,. She didn't even know his nationality as she described him as that 'funny little Frenchman'. Elizabeth Jones, the keeper of the lodging house, 'for ladies who received gentlemen' recalled that Muller had arrived at their place of business at about 9.30pm, to see Mary Ann, who was out with another 'gentleman'. The witness distinctly remembered that Miss Eldred had gone out thirty minutes earlier and had asked the time which, according to the kitchen clock, showed to be 9pm. If this testimony was true, Muller could not have travelled to Fenchurch Street in time to board the 'excursion to death' twenty minutes later. However, the 'alibi of the brothel clock that struck nine' from a woman who participated in the 'shameful trade' of the 'unfortunate class' was dismissed by the prosecution and the jury wasted no time in accepting the case against the defendant. On 1 November, three days after the end of his trial, Franz Muller wrote a letter in the condemned cell at Newgate Prison to his family in Germany, blaming his plight on a relationship with another girl - Grace Matthews, the sister of chief prosecution witness John Matthews:

Dearest Parents, Brothers and Sisters, Friends and Acquaintances, With trembling hand and sorrowful heart I take up the pen to give you further particulars of my misfortune, which in consequence of my disobedience towards you, dear parents, has followed me, and infinitely shortened the days of my life. I now plainly comprehend the sentence that stands written in the Bible - that whosoever does not honour his mother and father will be followed by an early death; but I only see it now when it is too late. I hope, nevertheless, that you who were so dear to me, will not discard me if all the world repulse me. ... I also hope you will forgive with all your hearts. I will now briefly tell

*you how it happened that I am overtaken by an unexpected death,
which, nevertheless, I do not deserve, but God oftentimes punishes
man by judgements which he does not deserve, and that is now the
case with me, in order to punish me for my evil deeds towards you, my
dearest parents; for had I listened to you and not proceeded to England
this misfortune would not have befallen me, but it is now too late, and
I will say no more on that subject but will describe how it came about.
I was acquainted with … Grace Matthews, and things proceeded so
far that I mediated marrying her.*

*As I was also acquainted with her brother, John Matthews, it
happened that he bought a hat for me. Through the purchase of this hat
he brought to me my unexpected death, as I had given up
acquaintanceship with his sister. On July 9, 1864, a man was
murdered in a railway carriage. From him a watch, chain, and hat
were taken from him at the same time, and another hat left in the
carriage, which hat was similar to the one John Matthews had bought
for me. A reward of 2,000 thalers* [units of German currency before
the introduction of the mark system] *was now offered for those
who could give information respecting the murder. I had long
previously resolved to go to America, as you yourselves know; and
therefore, on Monday July 11, 1864, I went towards the office to book
my passage to America, and on the way, a watch and chain were
offered to me, and I bought them, and as it afterwards appeared they
were the watch and chain belonging to the gentleman who was
murdered in the railway carriage on July 9, 1864.*

*I left London for America on July 14, 1864 and reached New York
on August 24, 1864, and was there arrested because John Matthews
had accused me of the murder, and consequently, I was brought back
to London. I could now not bring forward the man from whom I had
bought the watch and chain, and John Matthews swore that the hat
which was left in the carriage was the one he had bought for me on
October 24, 1863. I was now required to say where I was on July 9,
1864, and also what I did; yet the people said they could not remember,
which might easily be the case after so long a time, and on this account
I was found guilty of murder and sentenced to death; but God the
Almighty knows that I am innocent, and therefore I shall die in peace*

... as it is also said in the Holy Scripture: Fear not they who can kill the body, fear rather much more those who can destroy body and soul, and therefore I shall atone for my sins against you of which I have been guilty, and then the Lord will also graciously receive me.

Time has been left me till the 14 November, and therefore I write you some lines and send them as soon as possible in order that I may have peace, which I can only receive when you forgive me from your hearts, and that you will not refuse to me. In the hope that you will not let my request be uncomplied with, I remain, your loving son and brother, Franz Muller, who was sold as a slave in London by John Matthews for 2,000 thalers.

The convicted murderer kept up his protestation of innocence until moments before hangman William Calcraft was given the signal to carry out the public execution outside Newgate Gaol. Although, the correspondent of the *Daily News* reported that overnight, rain 'had a marked effect on attendance', causing the 'hot potato men and the girls who vended roast chestnut to complain bitterly about lack of trade', the *Annual Register* commented on the vulgar gathering of 'the lowest refuse of metropolitan life' that gradually built up to over 50,00 strong to watch the spectacle. In the case of Franz Muller, the traditional cry of 'Hats off', he's coming! - in order to settle the crowd and show some decorum for the imminent death of the condemned man as he mounted the scaffold, was supremely ironic. The vast crowd were herded into sheep pens, erected for the occasion as a form of crowd control, and the report in the *Daily News* described the reaction of the assembled 'mob':

It is quite true that the yells and shrieks, the bonneting and ticklings, the hat throwing and fighting, gave way for an instant for an intense desire to behold the sight, and that the immense concourse was momentarily hushed in the depth of its excitement and its anxiety to see all. But when the drop had fallen and the poor wretch was quivering in the air, there was a deep gasp as might come from a gourmand on tasting a rare dish, or a toper on quaffing a delicate wine. Next, the eager, staring, dreadfully hungry eyes, lost their fixity

Condemnation of FRANZ MULLER.

FAREWELL hope—all is despair !
No hope is left the murderer here :
Flight could not the murderer save,
Although he crossed the briny wave.
The brand of Cain was on his brow,
The past cannot be recalled now ;
Nothing now his life can save,
Muller is doomed to a murderer's grave.

Nothing on earth Muller's life can save,
From the scaffold and a murderer's grave
All escape for him has failed,
Even the ship could scarcely sail ;
Long days and nights of anguish led,
Always in fear, always in dread.
With blood-stained hands the blows were
        given,
He could not cast his eyes to Heaven ;
His innocence he still out-braved,
Yet Muller found a murderer's grave.

His aged victim looks from Heaven,
Prays for his murderer to be forgiven ;
Hurried from the world of woe,
In the midst of health, by that fatal blow.
By one so young, you'd scarce believe,
His artful ways could so deceive,
But the eye of God he could not brave,
Sentence of death and a murderer's grave

Mothers may weep for their children dear
But who for Muller will shed a tear ?
Perhaps far from friends and far from
        home,
In a loathsome cell, in anguish mourn.
Dark visions, perhaps, surround his bed.
In misery rests his weary head,
The love of gold made him its slave,
And brought him to a murderer's grave.

The sentence, Death, to him is given,
Prepare your soul for a place in Heaven,
Three weeks to live—how time will fly,
On the scaffold, Muller must die.
The time is given for him to live,
Is more than he gave to Mr. Briggs.
He is with angels, led by each hand,
Yet before Heaven's judgment Muller
        must stand.

Yes, he must suffer for his crime,
A young man scarcely in his prime ;
A few months back perhaps he was good,
His conscience free, on his soul no blood,
No one knows how his fate's decreed,
Perhaps to make our hearts to bleed,
Let us hope his soul he'll try to save—
Pray for a murderer when in his grave.

H. DISLEY, Printer, 57, High Street, St. Giles, London

A contemporary broadside lamenting the fate of Franz Muller.

of gaze, the craned necks were eased, and then by chatter, gibe, and grin, by delighted comparisons between the bearing of the man hung yesterday and the heroes of other executions, by hideous jests upon the dying man's agony, and by ribald mockery of the clergyman's prayers, did these pupils of the gallows show their appreciation of its lessons.

The instant the drop fell, there was a sensational development when the officiating chaplain, Dr Cappel, rushed from the scaffold, clasping his hands with great fervour, and exclaimed: 'Thank God, he's confessed, he's confessed'. The churchman later revealed the nature of a conversation in the final moments with the condemned man: 'Muller, I am about to leave you and you only have a few moments to live. I entreat you by the living God, before whom you will soon have to appear, to say whether you are guilty of this crime', to which Muller stubbornly replied, 'I am innocent'. Dr Cappel reiterated firmly, 'Innocent?' Muller then said, 'God only knows what I have done' It was then put to the prisoner, 'Does He know that you have committed this crime?' After a short pause, Muller finally conceded, 'I have done it and no-one else'. The relieved churchman barely had time to utter 'Then may God have mercy upon your soul' before William Calcraft drew the bolt to complete 'his dreadful duty'.

Franz Muller's ultimate fate had been decreed before his trial by eminent author and social reformer Charles Dickens. Despite being a vehement critic of public executions, the writer discussed the ill-feeling he felt toward the railway carriage murderer in a letter to a friend:

I hope that the gentlemen [Muller] will be hanged, and have hardly a doubt of it, though croakers contrariwise are not wanting. It is difficult to conceive any other line of defence than the circumstances proved, taken separately, are slight. But a sound Judge will immediately charge the jury that the strength of the circumstances lies in their being put together and will thread them together on a fatal rope.

The Brighton Carriage Murder

Railway murderer Franz Muller used his skills as a tailor to reduce the size of his victim's top hat by cutting it down and stitching it to the rim. This started a craze among fashion-conscious young men of the day who began to copy the style and wear hats known as a 'Muller'. When the 'Brighton Railway Tragedy' became Britain's second railway murder case, the defendant, Percy Lefroy, an unsuccessful freelance journalist with theatrical pretensions, whose real name was Arthur Lefroy Mapleton, asked for permission to wear full evening dress in court as he believed his smart appearance would impress the judge and jury at his trial. This request was refused, although, the prisoner was allowed to carry his new hat. During the legal proceedings the accused stood in the dock continually cleaning, examining and contemplating the shiny silk topper, seemingly unperturbed by the seriousness of the situation and the grave charges he faced of knifing and shooting elderly Isaac Frederick Gold in a first class railway carriage on the London, Brighton & South Coast Railway.

On the afternoon of 27 June 1881, the victim had put up a terrific struggle, seen fleetingly by a female witness living in a trackside cottage, before being overpowered and robbed of a few coins and his watch. The life and death struggle had lasted for several miles of the journey before sixty-four-year-old Mr Gold succumbed with fourteen knife wounds and was jettisoned out of the moving train. His lifeless body was later recovered near the entrance to Balcombe Tunnel on the line running between London Bridge and Brighton.

Travelling as a passenger in the same carriage was Percy Lefroy who staggered on to the station platform when he alighted at Preston Park. Suffering with head injuries and wearing heavily bloodstained clothes, he appeared dazed and confused and told a ticket collector that he had been travelling in the first class compartment with two strangers. As the train entered Mertsham Tunnel he heard a shot, was attacked in the dark, then knocked out under a barrage of blows. When the badly injured man awoke, bleeding profusely and lying on the floor, he found himself alone in the carriage and, much later, following the discovery of the victim's body, insisted he was totally unaware that a more serious crime had been committed during the period he was rendered unconscious. Furthermore, the suspect insisted that the real assailant must have been the 'other passenger', whom he described as a rough-looking, bewhiskered character, aged about fifty years and, from observing his rural appearance 'probably a countryman'.

Before the mangled corpse of Isaac Gold was found by a railway ganger, the police thought that Lefroy had concocted the story to cover-up a failed attempt by himself to commit suicide. However, as the victim's missing gold watch and chain was spotted by railway staff, partially hidden and protruding carelessly from Lefroy's boot, and the defendant suspiciously absconded when released by the police until further inquiries were made, this alibi of the 'third man' did not impress the jury at his subsequent murder trial and they returned their inevitable verdict after a deliberation of only ten minutes.

At Maidstone Assizes, the trial judge, Lord Chief Justice Coleridge, was equally dismissive of the twenty-one-year-old defendant: 'You have been convicted on the clearest evidence of a most ferocious murder, a murder perpetrated on a harmless old man, who had done you no wrong; he was perhaps unknown to you. You have justly and rightfully been convicted, and it is right and just that you should die'. Sentenced to death, Lefroy, keeping up the pretence that the 'wrong man' was in the dock, turned to the jury and said, 'Gentlemen, some day when it is too late, you will learn that you have murdered me'.

As his execution loomed, however, and no reprieve was forthcoming, the agitated prisoner was questioned by his solicitor in the condemned cell, and finally made a series of garbled confessions on the day before he was hanged by William Marwood at Lewes Prison on 29 November 1881.

The trial of Percy Lefroy.

Press reports revealed that Percy Lefroy gave five different accounts of the manner in which he robbed and killed Isaac Gold. One version of events proffered to his solicitor indicated that he had acted in self-defence and that his victim had initiated the violent confrontation.

According to Lefroy, he had been moving in social circles he could not afford in an effort to be accepted among the theatrical and literary set - a lifestyle that had left him facing bankruptcy. Therefore, on the morning of the murder, he redeemed a pistol from a pawnbroker, then boarded the train in search of easy pickings at London Bridge. He considered robbing a gentleman passenger, before changing his mind and moving to the compartment occupied by Mr Gold when the train stopped at Croydon Following a brief conversation between the two men, the intended victim put down the newspaper he was reading to have a doze. To shield his eyes from the light and enable him to sleep, he placed a handkerchief over his eyes. As the handkerchief was pulled from his pocket, it accidentally drew out his purse which fell onto the floor of the compartment. Lefroy instantly threw his own handkerchief over the purse and bent down to steal it, but was seen and challenged, 'You scoundrel. Do you want to rob me?' Mr Gold then punched the thief and sent him sprawling across the carriage, revealing the butt end of the pistol concealed in the thief's inside breast pocket. Realising that Lefroy was armed, Mr Gold shouted, 'You villain, is it murder as well as robbery that you intend?'

Rushing at Lefroy, the angry passenger seized the gun and fired twice without causing any harm. Lefroy snatched back the firearm and retaliated by firing two shots at Mr Gold. One bullet missed while the other inflicted a wound in the victim's neck. The two men fought savagely and Lefroy received gun butt wounds to his scalp that were later dressed by a doctor at Brighton.

The murderer, rather improbably, claimed that his victim produced a penknife from his pocket with one hand, while pinning Lefroy to the floor with the other hand around his throat, then, opening the blade with his teeth, the exhausted elderly man, suffering from blood loss, was disarmed as his strength failed him. Repeatedly stabbed in the face, neck and arms as he tried to ward off the blows, the bitter struggle came to an end when Isaac Gold was pushed out of the door, still alive, clinging by his fingernails to the running board of the carriage. The killer also flung the weapons and the dead man's hat on to the track. The hat was found ten miles away from the body, providing conclusive proof to the police that, as the train had not stopped anywhere else along that stretch of rail, the murderer was still in the same blood splattered compartment when it came to a halt at Preston Park, giving the lie to the plausible story quickly thought up by the killer to explain his battered and bloodied appearance.

Percy Lefroy's legal team made a belated appeal for clemency on the grounds of insanity as their client also confessed to a murder that he clearly did not commit. The alleged victim was army officer, Lt Percy Roper, who had been shot at his barracks earlier that year. Lefroy claimed he had killed Roper for insulting the good name of a well-known actress of the day, Violet Cameron. Infatuated with this lady, Lefroy carried a picture

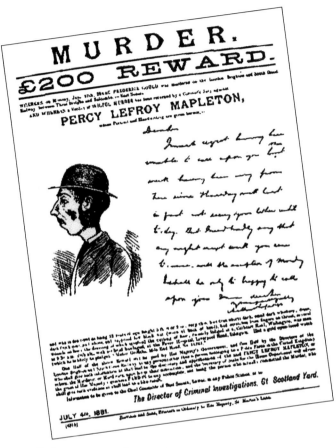

Lefroy was on the run for a month.

of her on his person and the deluded suitor had even told family members that she was married to him. When initially questioned on the day of the murder, Lefroy told police that Miss Cameron had been due to travel with him to Brighton where he had an appointment to discuss the production of his new play with theatre manager Mrs Nye Chart at the prestigious Theatre Royal and Opera House. It transpired that neither of the two ladies knew him and, when Lefroy subsequently went on the run for a month until arrested, the police were to rue the fact that they had not checked out this fantasy before releasing him.

Languishing in the condemned cell, Lefroy wrote a letter to the object of his affection, Violet Cameron, claiming that they had been introduced while she was appearing at a Brighton theatre in 1878. According to Lefroy's recollection, she had presented him with the 'most treasured possession I have in the world - a faded rose you carelessly gave to me'. The following extract is from the 'most painful and unaccountable' letter received by the actress and published in the *Daily Telegraph*:

Actress Violet Cameron.

It was a love that has been the mainspring of my life ever since. Hopeless, unrequited as it might be, it was an intense, honest passion, and as such has saved me from many and many a sin I should otherwise have committed. From a distance I have watched you rise in your profession with mingled feelings. Feelings of delight, and at the same time of bitter despair. Delight at your well-deserved success; despair as every upward step you took widened the gulf between us. But all the time I have lived on with the wild vague hope of winning you in the end. Trying to do right for your sake. And as you, with the world at your feet, loved by many and admired by all who know you and your brave unselfish life in your danger set profession accept this last tribute, small and worthless though it may seem, of gratitude, aye, and hopeless love, from one whose life is quickly closing in. You have always been my ideal of what a woman should be. Your face as I first saw is ever at my side, aye, and will be to the bitter end.

It emerged that on one occasion, a hoax letter which, later proved to be in Lefroy's handwriting, had been received by Violet Cameron urging her to visit a relative of hers, theatre manager Alexander

Henderson who had, purportedly, been seriously injured. Lefroy's plan to lure the actress to meet him was uncovered when the cabman who delivered the message revealed that his instructions were to convey her to London Bridge terminus. These strange confessions and revelations prompted defence solicitor, Mr T.D. Dutton, to believe that the convicted murderer was 'as mad as mad could be'. However, a plea for his client to be reprieved was dismissed by Sir William Harcourt, the Home Secretary, whose view of the case was shared wholeheartedly in a summary published in this editorial comment in the Sunday periodical *Reynolds Newspaper*:

If ever a man deserved to suffer a violent death at the hands of his fellow men it was the atrocious scoundrel who was hanged at Lewes. Our readers know full well that we are opposed to capital punishment. We do not hold with the savage interpretation placed by the Church and Society on the scriptural injunction that 'whoso sheddeth man's blood by man shall his blood be shed'. The fallibility of human judgement would of itself, if no other arguments were forthcoming, constitute a protest against the hangman's office, But so long as that exists - so long as the gallows is a national institution, there cannot be a doubt that no one has ever suffered thereon more deservedly than Lefroy Mapleton. He was a vulgar, commonplace scoundrel, a combination of ruffianism and self-conceit, and altogether a fellow for whom little or no sympathy could be entertained. He had a wonderful faculty for lying.

The murder he perpetrated was a premeditated, and to some extent, cleverly contrived crime; insomuch as the victim he selected was an elderly, well-to-do looking person, a comfortable old gentleman who was certain to have in his possession a certain amount of money, and likewise, in all probability a valuable watch. Lefroy, like Muller, who murdered Mr Biggs on the North London Railway, took good stock of his purposed prey; and both laid their plans accordingly. Neither was mad; but murderers of the most dangerous type. In all probability Mr Gold offered a more desperate and determined resistance to the sudden attempt of Lefroy than did Mr Briggs to that of his German assailant. And hence it was the more surprising that the Brighton police

The execution of Percy Lefroy.

temporarily released a person who not only told them an improbable tale, but also bore upon his person all the evidences of a formidable fray.

There was in fact no defence for the prisoner. The whole story presented itself to the unprejudiced view of every sane person in all its ghastly stages. There was the penniless desperado who had pawned his last valuable for the express purpose of purchasing a first-class ticket for Brighton, lurking on the railway platform in search of an eligible looking victim. There was Mr Gold, a well dressed, well-to-do person, ensconced alone in the corner of the carriage, into which Lefroy followed him. When his fellow passenger's eyes were covered with his handkerchief, he was suddenly assailed, and commenced the hand-to-hand struggle for life which was witnessed from the window of a cottage by which the train passed. Ultimately Mr Gold succumbed, and his body either fell or was thrown out of the carriage on to the rails. All this presents itself to the mind's eye of every rational person as the main incidents of what occurred on the occasion of Mr Gold's last and fatal journey to his home near Brighton.

The defence of insanity, even if set up, could have availed nothing. There was far too much method in the means Lefroy adopted to replenish his empty purse by the contents of Mr Gold's to admit of any such plea being accepted. Up to a certain time, the murderer, who seems to have something of the mountebank in his composition, posed for the public. His attitudes at Maidstone had all been carefully studied, and the nonchalance with which he regarded the proceedings upon which his life hung was altogether assumed. When, however, the hour of his doom approached - when, as it were, the shadow of Marwood, the executioner, was darkening the portals of his prison cell, then the self-possession of the criminal entirely abandoned him; his demeanour and behaviour suddenly changed. He was no longer tranquil or resigned, but raved like a wild beast. Anything to obtain even the slightest chance of a reprieve - to procrastinate the dread moment when the halter was around his neck. To proclaim himself the perpetrator of another murder might serve this end; and in all likelihood, according to what was passing through his fevered imagination, the Home Secretary would be so staggered by this self-denunciation, that an immediate respite must be granted in order to inquire into the circumstances of the case. But Sir William Harcourt was not to be thus led astray. The farce following the tragedy was played out, and Lefroy was duly executed.

None but a maniac or a mad doctor will for an instant raise any doubt as to his sanity. And none but the most credulous of simpletons can place the slightest faith in his bogus confession of the murder of Lieutenant Roper. That was the last effort of a dastardly wretch to avoid the punishment the law of his country had awarded for one of the foulest crimes that is recorded in its criminal history.

Jack the Ripper on the Underground

During the Nineteenth Century, the horror that gripped the public imagination during the media frenzy that accompanied the railway murders committed by Franz Muller and Percy Lefroy was surpassed by only one series of crimes - 'The Whitechapel Murders' - featuring the most infamous serial killer in history - 'Jack the Ripper'. Although, never identified, the serial killer has often been depicted as a 'swell' attired in full evening dress of silk topper, neck-tie, cloak, suit and patent leather shoes as he terrorised 'ladies of the night'. The atrocities took place in the heart of London's East End where homicide was commonplace, yet, the sheer ferocity and savagery inflicted on the victims immediately attracted lurid headlines in the press as five prostitutes were killed and mutilated over a three-month period in the Autumn of 1888.

The first of these so-called 'canonical' victims was struck down on 31 August, when the body of Mary 'Polly' Nichols was found. Unable to afford a bed in a lodging house, she had been wandering the streets trying to raise money by prostitution when her throat was viciously cut right through to the spinal column before her skirts were raised and her abdomen ripped open exposing her intestines. A week later, a street girl with a bad temper and black moods known as 'Dark Annie' Chapman met a similar fate, when her intestines were removed and laid neatly on the ground, while her womb was removed and taken away by her killer.

Jack the Ripper struck fives times in three months.

On the last day of September, an infamous 'double event' occurred when two women were slain in a single night. Elizabeth 'Long Liz' Stride was last seen talking to a man 'respectable' in appearance - less than thirty minutes before her body was discovered. This time there was no mutilation and blood was still seeping from the dead woman's throat, indicating that Jack the Ripper had narrowly escaped detection. Forty minutes later, the psychopath struck again and killed Catherine 'Kate' Eddowes. With maniacal zeal, her throat, face and abdomen were slashed and a kidney and womb removed. The worst atrocity was saved for the final victim Mary Jane Kelly who was attacked in her lodging house on 9 November 1888. When a rent collector called on the streetwalker, he peeped through the window and spotted her naked, bloodied corpse lying on the bed. Her face had been brutalised almost beyond recognition; flesh removed from her abdomen and thighs was found on a bedside table, while the breasts

The fate of Annie Chapman.

had been sliced off and her heart extracted and removed from the scene of the crime. The shocked witness who made the terrible discovery remarked 'It looked more like the work of a devil than a man'.

Letters sent to a news agency were signed by the self-proclaimed 'Jack the Ripper' and a prominent London citizen received a piece of kidney which the writer claimed he had taken from one of the dead women, boasting - 'tother I fried and ate' - in correspondence purportedly received 'From Hell'. Such psychopaths are usually compelled to continue their killing spree until they are apprehended, but following the death of the fifth victim, the murderer's reign of terror mysteriously ceased and the villain was never brought to justice.

Since the time of the atrocities, numerous suspects, accomplices and conspirators have continually been named in connection with the crime. These include members of the royal family Edward, Prince of Wales and his eldest son, Prince Albert Victor, prominent politicians William Gladstone and Randolph Churchill, eminent artists Walter Sickert and Frank Miles, poets James Kenneth Stephen and Algernon Swinburne, writers George Gissing and Lewis

Carroll, physicians Sir William Gull and Sir Arthur Conan Doyle. However, it can be argued that such famous personalities would have been easily recognised and it has been proposed that the crimes could have been committed by someone in uniform who would not raise suspicion, such as a soldier, sailor or policeman. In recent years, a retired former Metropolitan Police Officer Bernard Brown, formulated an intriguing theory linking the murders to an employee of the railway. Furthermore, he asserted his belief that the killer may have provided an hitherto overlooked clue to his identity when, on 27th September 1888, the Central News Agency received a letter which began:

Dear Boss
I keep hearing the Police have caught me, but they won't fix me just yet. I have laughed when they look so clever and talk about being on the right track.

If Bernard Brown's theory is correct, the last phrase provides a vital clue as to why the blood-stained murderer was able to escape time and time again from an area heavily patrolled by the police and members of a local vigilante committee. The answer is that all the crimes were committed in the immediate vicinity of a railway line. The police might well have been on the right 'track' if they had investigated the possibility that the villain was a railway policeman who avoided detection by fleeing to the nearest underground station of the Metropolitan Railway which, coincidentally, was celebrating its Jubilee. The first section opened in 1863, when, in addition to the principal terminal stations at Paddington and Holborn, 'commodious' passenger stations were erected serving Edgware Road, Regents Park, Hampstead Road, Euston Square and Kings Cross.

By 1884, the underground line of the Metropolitan Railway had extended to Whitechapel and Mile End. While above ground, the Whitechapel Railway Station, operated by the East London Railway, also served trains operated by the Great Eastern Railway, the South Eastern Railway, and the London, Brighton and South Coast

A London underground station - a cross section.

Railway. All five railway companies assigned police officers to the area who wore uniforms similar to London 'bobbies'. Patrolling the Whitechapel railway and underground stations and Spitalfields Goods Yard, the railway policemen could only be recognised from one another by their individual company arms displayed on their helmets and uniforms. Prior to the opening of the 'underground communication' in January 1863, the *Illustrated London News* described the reasoning behind the scheme adopted by the Metropolitan Company as a means 'by which the most densely crowded districts could be traversed without the slightest annoyance of obstruction' - a system that may have made it possible for Jack the Ripper to come and go at will, or, as a report in the *Times* observed, 'free from any fear of interruption while on his dreadful work'.

Initially, the Metropolitan Railway was to be worked by a revolutionary form of steam locomotive using hot firebricks instead of a coal fire to heat the engine boiler. Known as 'Fowler's Ghost' (named after the company engineer), the small firebox of the new design failed to generate enough steam, therefore, tank engines were fitted with surface condensers to consume the smoke and exhaust emitted by the locomotive. In addition, maintenance shafts known as 'blowholes' were inserted from the roadway to the underground railway to allow the noxious fumes to escape. These same shafts would have also given the serial killer access to the tunnels without running the risk of mixing with members of the public or railway staff on an actual station. At the height of the murder scare, the *Illustrated Police News* published an amusing cartoon showing Jack the Ripper descending the Tower Subway that runs beneath the River Thames from Tower Hill. Unwittingly, Bernard Brown notes, the artist revealed a possible route for the killer. The southern exit of the subway leads into Bermondsey, thence to the railway terminus at London Bridge, where the 'Railway Ripper' could easily blend in unnoticed amongst the policemen of the South East Railway and London Brighton & South Coast Railway before travelling to the killing ground of Whitechapel via New Cross.

Jack the Ripper's possible route via the subway at Tower Bridge.

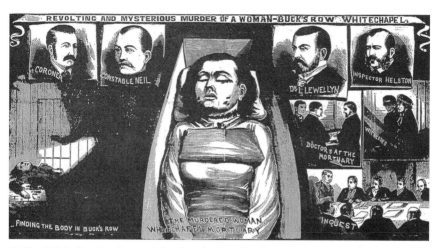

Polly Nichols, the first of the five 'canonical' victims.

News of the death of the first victim, Polly Nichols, whose body was found mutilated behind Whitechapel Underground Station in Bucks Row, was telegraphed to Scotland Yard by the police of 'J' Division stationed at Bethnal Green. Following the 'double-event' killing of Elizabeth Stride and Catherine Eddowes, a baffling graffiti message appeared scrawled on a wall near the murder scene that purportedly read: 'The Juwes are not the men that will be blamed for nothing'. A policeman from 'A' Division in Whitehall, PC Alfred Long, an unreliable witness who was later dismissed from the force for drunkenness, was the officer that deciphered the word 'Juwes'. Scotland Yard commissioner, Sir Charles Warren, immediately ordered the writing to be removed and refused to allow it to be photographed, which brought this stinging criticism in the form of a verse published in the periodical *Fun*:

> *Some horrid murders have been done*
> *All in the slums of Whitechapel*
> *The 'Bobbies' up and down have run*
> *To find a clue, but sad to tell,*
> *The only link, a written scrawl*

Too early in the dawning day;
It was upon a dirty wall,
Some busybody wiped away.

Sir Charles Warren acted hastily, believing that the phrase 'Juwes' was a misspelling of the word 'Jews'. Such a slur could have stirred up anti-Semitic feeling in the district where railway notices were displayed on the underground in Yiddish to keep the large Jewish population informed. However, the graffiti appeared near the old Aldgate East Station which provided a convenient escape route for Jack the Ripper. It is possible that the fleeing killer paused briefly to taunt the police further by writing, 'The Jayes are not the men that will be blamed for nothing' - a reference to 'J' Division police who patrolled the Whitechapel area and had failed to find the killer of Polly Nicholls. Furthermore, during the investigation, detectives from 'J' Division conducted a fruitless search for evidence along the East London and District Railway station and embankments - virtually an impossible task as the entire system lay in tunnels below the surface. This line of inquiry was unwittingly alluded to in the first line of the second stanza in the following extract from a contemporary broadside ballad:

Now ladies all beware or you'll get caught in a snare,
They seem to say the devil's running loose,
With a big knife in his hand, he trots throughout the land,
And with all the ladies means to play the deuce

Now they've searched the underground, and all the country round,
In every hole and corner so they say,
But he comes out of a night, and puts us in a fright,
And he manages somehow to get away.

'Saucy Jack' may have given another vital clue in a letter to the police considered a hoax at the time. Postmarked 'Liverpool' and dated 28 September, the contents of the letter warned, 'Beware I shall be at work on the first and second in the Minories at 12 midnight and I give the authorities a good chance, but there is never a policeman near when I am at work'. Bernard Brown believes that the killer was indicating that the murders had taken place in the vicinity of a fixed point where a policeman was normally stationed. When the officers went off duty at 1am - the murderer began his grisly night's work. If these hours had been extended by Sir Charles Warren during the reign of terror, it might have led to the capture of Jack the Ripper. A fixed point existed outside Whitechapel Station just the other side of the railway line where the body of Polly Nicholls was found.. Annie Chapman's corpse was discovered at 29 Hanbury Street, Spitalfields, a few yards away from yet another fixed point in Hanbury Street, just a short distance from Brick Lane where Shoreditch Underground Station offered refuge for the murderer.

On 30 September, two days after the letter had been sent predicting that he would strike on the 'first and second' of October, the infamous 'double event' took place. Elizabeth Stride's body was found in Dutfield's Yard, Berner Street, once again just minutes away from a fixed point in Commercial Road, at the junction with Christian Street. At that time, there was a nearby Metropolitan

Catherine Eddowes.

District Railway Station situated on the south side of Whitechapel Road known as St. Mary's. From here, it would have been possible to travel underground to Aldgate Station, near Mitre Square, where Catherine Eddowes died within an hour of Elizabeth Stride. On 9 November, Mary Jane Kelly, the last of the five 'canonical' victims, was found mutilated beyond recognition at her lodgings in Millers Court, Dorset Street, just yards from a fixed point outside Spitalfields Church. On this occasion, ongoing tramway works throughout the night posed a problem for Jack the Ripper as to which escape route to use.

The most convenient routes - north to Shoreditch Station or south to Aldgate East - were too risky. His only alternative was to travel west and disappear to the depths of Bishopsgate Metropolitan Underground Station, which lay beneath the new Liverpool Street terminus.

Although, there is general consensus among modern-day 'Ripperogists' that Polly Nichols, Annie Chapman, Elizabeth Stride, Catherine Eddowes and Mary Jane Kelly are the only genuine victims of Jack the Ripper, it has been argued that an indefinite number of the murders are, or, are not, attributable to one man.

Frances Coles' body was found below a railway arch.

Estimates of the names of other possible victims by the same killer vary wildly from as few as three to as many as thirty committed in the area over a number of years before, during, and after 1888. Bernard Brown offers similar convincing solutions pointing to the killer being a railway policemen in several unsolved murder cases including the deaths of 'Fairy' Kay (denounced by many experts as a 'mythical victim' supposedly killed at Mitre Square on Boxing Day 1887), Martha Tabram (attacked in George's Yard, Whitechapel Road, she had been

Frances Coles.

stabbed 39 times, August 1888), Alice McKenzie (aka Clay Pipe Alice, found with her throat cut and a knife wound from left breast to navel, July 1889) Rose Mylett (strangled with cord, December 1889), Elizabeth Jackson (remains washed up on the banks of the Thames, June 1889) and Frances Coles (aka Carroty Nell, found dying with her throat cut beneath railway arches in February1891).

Summarising his remarkable theory, Bernard Brown, does not accuse, though, none to subtly hints, that the perpetrator of the 'Whitechapel Murders' may have been one of two former railway employees who were also directly involved in the official police investigation into the unfathomable mystery of Jack the Ripper:

This then is how I believe the murders were committed, and how the Ripper got away completely unobserved. I do not intend to suggest the identity of the Ripper, only his profession. However two senior investigating officers on the Ripper enquiry came from a railway background. Inspector Richard Webb of 'J' Division (Bethnal Green) had formerly been with the Great Western Railway (GWR) and Inspector Henry Moore of the CID at Scotland Yard, son of a Met officer, had been a clerk with the South Eastern Railway (SER) (whose trains ran through Whitechapel). They both retired in 1899, Moore taking up a position of Superintendent of the Great Eastern Railway Company. It was beneath GER arches that Coles, the Ripper's final victim had been found.

Bibliography and Sources

General Sources
Crime and Criminals, London, W& R Chambers Ltd. 2002
Flanders, Judith. *The Invention of Murder*, London, Harper Press 2011
Gaute, J.H.H. O'Dell, Robin. *The Murderer's Who's Who*, London, Pan Books 1980
Matthew, H.C.G. and Harris, Brian (eds). *Oxford Dictionary of National Biography*, Oxford University Press, 2004
Website sources:
British Transport Police:
Nineteenth Century Newspapers: http://infotrac.galegroup.com
Times Digital Archive: http://infotrac.galegroup.com
Wikipedia the free encyclopedia: www.wikipedia.org

Great Train Robberies

The Great Western Railway Robberies
Holgate, Mike. *Murder & Mystery on the Great Western Railway*, Wellington, Halsgrove 2006
Journals and Periodicals:
Exeter Gazette, Trewman's Exeter Flying Post, Taunton Courier Times, Manchester Times, The Times,
The Bermondsey Murder
Alpert, Michael. *London 1849*, Harlow, Pearson Education Ltd., 2004
Boase, G.C. *Manning, Marie*, in Oxford Dictionary of National

Biography, Matthew, H.C.G. and Harris, Brian (eds). Oxford University Press, 2004

Borowitz, Albert. *The Bermondsey Horror*, London, Robson Books 1988

Huish, Robert. *The Progress of Crime or the Authentic Memoirs of Maria Manning*, London 1849

Journals and Periodicals:
Illustrated London News, Lloyds Weekly News

The Great Bullion Robbery
Crichton, Michael. *The Great Train Robbery*, London, Bantam Books 1976

Journals and Periodicals:
British Transport Journal, The Era, Lloyd's Weekly News, Morning Post, Penny Illustrated, The Times

The Great Train Robbery
Crime and Criminals, London, W& R Chambers Ltd. 2002

Biggs, Ronnie. *Odd Man Out: The Last Straw*, London, M Press (Media) Ltd. 2011.

Holgate, Mike. *Devon Villains, Rogues, Rascals and Reprobates*, Stroud, The History Press 2011

Reynolds, Bruce. *Autobiography of a Thief*, London, Corgi 1995

Journals and Periodicals:
Daily Mail, Daily Mirror, Herald Express (South Devon), Illustrated London News, London Evening Standard, The Times

Crime on the Royal Road

The Slough Murder

Head, Francis Bond, Sir, Bart. *Stokers and Pokers*, London, John Murray 1849

MacDermot, E.T. *History of the Great Western Railway, Vol.2 1833-1863*, London, Great Western Railway Company, 1931

Williams, Archibald. *Brunel and After: The Romance of the Great Western Railway,* London, The Great Western Railway, 1925
Journals and Periodicals:
The Globe, Illustrated London News, The Sun, Sydney Gazette, The Times, Windsor and Eaton Express
Queen Victoria's Station Assassin
Matthew, H.C.G. Reynolds, K.D. *Queen Victoria* in *Oxford Dictionary of National Biography,* Matthew, H.C.G. and Harris, Brian (eds), Oxford University Press, 2004
Sellwood, Arthur & Mary. *The Victorian Railway Murders,* Newton Abbot, David & Charles, 1979
Strachey, Lytton. *Queen Victoria,* London, Bloomsbury 1921
Weintraub, Stanley. *Victoria: Biography of A Queen,* London, Unwin Hyman 1987
Journals and Periodicals:
Daily News, Illustrated London News, Leicester Chronicle, Morning Post, Penny Illustrated, The Star, The Times

First Class Railway Murders

The First Railway Carriage Murder
Gaute, J.H.H. O'Dell, Robin. *The Murderer's Who's Who,* London, Pan Books 1980
Sellwood, Arthur & Mary. *The Victorian Railway Murders,* Newton Abbot, David & Charles, 1979
Journals and Periodicals:
Daily News, Lloyd's Weekly News, Morning Post, Penny Illustrated, The Times
The Brighton Carriage Murder
Foulkes, Richard. *Violet Cameron* in *Oxford Dictionary of National Biography,* Matthew, H.C.G. and Harris, Brian (eds), Oxford University Press, 2004

Sellwood, Arthur & Mary. *The Victorian Railway Murders*, Newton Abbot, David & Charles, 1979

Journals and Periodicals:

Daily News, Daily Telegraph, Freeman's Journal, Illustrated Police News, Penny Illustrated News, Reynold's Newspaper, The Star, Sussex Express

Jack the Ripper on the Underground

Begg, Paul, Fido, Martin, Skinner, Keith. *The Jack the Ripper A-Z, London*, Headline Publishing 1991

Brown, Bernard. *Was Jack the Ripper a Railway Policeman?* Journal of the Police History Society 2006

Davenport-Hines, Richard. *Jack the Ripper* in *Oxford Dictionary of National Biography*, Matthew, H.C.G. and Harris, Brian (eds), Oxford University Press, 2004

Holgate, Mike. *Jack the Ripper: The Celebrity Suspects*, The History Press, 2008

Website sources:

British Transport Police:

Casebook: Jack the Ripper: www.casebook.org

Journals and Periodicals:

Fun, Illustrated London News, Illustrated Police News, Punch, The Times